“THEY TAKE OUR JOBS!”

"THEY TAKE OUR JOBS!"

And 20 Other Myths about Immigration

AVIVA CHOMSKY

BEACON PRESS
BOSTON

BEACON PRESS
25 Beacon Street
Boston, Massachusetts 02108-2892
www.beacon.org

Beacon Press books
are published under the auspices of
the Unitarian Universalist Association of Congregations.

Printed in the United States of America

10 09 08 8 7 6 5 4 3

This book is printed on acid-free paper that meets the uncoated paper
ANSI/NISO specifications for permanence as revised in 1992.

Composition by Wilsted & Taylor Publishing Services

LIBRARY OF CONGRESS CATALOGING-IN-PUBLICATION DATA
Chomsky, Aviva.
"They take our jobs!": and 20 other myths about immigration / Aviva Chomsky.
p. cm.
Includes bibliographical references.
ISBN 978-0-8070-4156-7
1. United States—Emigration and immigration—Public opinion. 2. United States—Emigration and immigration—Government policy. 3. Immigrants—United States—Public opinion. 4. Public opinion—United States. I. Title.

JV6455.C46 2007
304.8'73—dc22 2007005025

CONTENTS

A NOTE ON TERMINOLOGY

Migration/immigration. Migration refers to any movement of humans (or animals) from one area to another. Immigration refers to such movements by humans when they involve crossing established state boundaries and are regulated by the governments of the territories they involve. So immigration really exists only under the modern state system.

First World/Third World. The term "third world" was coined in the 1950s as part of an anticolonial analysis that explained the poverty of many of the world's regions as a legacy of their colonial past. It contrasted the situation of the former colonies to that of the "first world" industrialized powers, and the "second world," or socialist bloc, countries.

Modernization theorists compared "underdeveloped" or "less developed" countries to "developed" countries, implying that "development" was a discrete process that all countries would go through at their own pace. Scholars from the dependency school responded that underdevelopment and development were two sides of the same coin: underdevelopment was not a starting state but rather a result of colonial exploitation. Walter Rodney's *How Europe Underdeveloped Africa* critiques the term and the theory behind it.

Other economists offered "industrialized" and "non-industrialized," and later added "newly industrialized" or NICS (newly industrialized countries, referring usually to Singapore, South Korea, Taiwan, and Hong Kong). But the deindustrialization of the first world, and the very different nature of the industrialization now going on in the third, makes these terms problematic.

Despite the radical changes in the global economic and social order since the 1950s, the concepts of First World and Third World still offer considerable power for understanding the roots and nature of global inequality.

Latino/Hispanic. Although the terms are often used interchangeably today, they have very different histories. Most people of Latin American origin in the United States have historically identified themselves ethnically by the country they come from (i.e., as Mexican, Dominican, Colombian, etc.). During the 1960s, in the context of anticolonial revolutions abroad and African American and Native American organizing at home, a Chicano movement and a Puerto Rican or Boricua movement also emerged in the United States. These movements identified with the indigenous peoples of their homelands. "Chicano" referred to Mexican Americans' ancestry among the Mexica indigenous people; "Boricua" referred to the Taíno name for the island of Puerto Rico. They used the concept of internal colonialism and analyzed their historical situation in the United States as that of colonized minorities, rather than immigrants.

It was in this context that the U.S. government began

to utilize the term "Hispanic." To some, especially in the Southwest, it was a term that tried to depoliticize their identity, and in particular to erase the indigenous and African origins of many Latin Americans. In the Mexican North (now the U.S. Southwest), "Hispanic" tended to be used by Spanish-origin elites to distinguish themselves from Mexicans of African and indigenous origin, and many Chicano activists found the term offensive. On the East Coast, where Puerto Rican migrants saw their country's resistance to Anglicization as an important part of their identity and ethnic pride, the term "Hispanic" tended to be taken on more readily as an acknowledgment of the importance of the Spanish language to Puerto Ricans.

"Latino" came into common usage in the 1980s, as an alternative to "Hispanic." More Latin Americans from different parts of the continent were entering the United States, and people of Mexican and Puerto Rican origin were becoming more and more geographically dispersed throughout the country. The term "Latino" grew out of the same political consciousness as "Chicano" and "Boricua," but expanded it to all Latin Americans, acknowledging the common historical experience of colonization and oppression of people of Latin American origin in the United States.

By the year 2000, though, the term "Latino" had lost much of its radical edge. Mainstream newspapers began to adopt it, and the 2000 census offered "Hispanic or Latino" as a category.

Some scholars and activists point out a further awkwardness built into the term "Hispanic": because it encompasses all things (or people) related to Spain or the Spanish language, it creates a category of people that includes those from a European country—Spain—and Spanish-speaking Latin America, but not people from Brazil or Haiti. It might be a logical category for studying literature ("Hispanic literature"), but it is not one that makes a lot of sense in looking at immigrants or ethnicity in the United States.

INTRODUCTION

Today's immigration debate is rife with myths, stereotypes, and unquestioned assumptions. I—and we all—hear remarks such as: "Immigrants take our jobs and drive down wages." "Why don't they learn English?" or "I'm not against immigration, only illegal immigration." After twenty years of teaching, writing, and organizing about immigration, it's clear to me that many of the arguments currently being circulated are based on serious misconceptions not only about how our society and economy function, but also about the history of immigration, the law, and the reasons for immigration.

All you have to do is read the papers or listen to the radio to notice that people seem to be extremely distraught and angry about immigration. Immigrants are blamed for a host of social ills and compared unfavorably to previous generations of immigrants. Since they are legally deprived of many of the rights that U.S. citizens enjoy, including the right to vote, elected officials and the general public can marginalize, blame, punish, and discriminate against them with little repercussion. Noncitizens make easy targets and convenient scapegoats.

A lot of our assumptions and opinions about immigration today are based on a set of beliefs about this country's past. These beliefs are formed by our social studies and history classes, by our textbooks, by our politicians, and by our media—indeed they are so pervasive that they almost permeate the air we breathe. Yet they are also fundamentally distorted. They represent a sanitized version of history that can undermine our ability to analyze the world we live in today. In analyzing the issues surrounding immigration today, this book will often turn to the past to revise some of the fallacies that have shaped the way we view our society.

Most U.S. citizens believe that this country is founded on principles of equal rights. They acknowledge that throughout history many groups were excluded from access to rights —Native Americans, people of African origin, women. But the story of U.S. history is generally told as one of gradual expansion of rights to new groups of people, until finally, with the civil rights legislation of the 1960s, the last remnants of discrimination and exclusion were presumably removed.

To those included in the circle of rights, the exclusion of others has always seemed justified, so much so as to be virtually beyond the bounds of discussion. When the founding fathers wrote that "all men are created equal" it was quite obvious to them that women were *not* created equal to men, and that "all men" meant "white men."

When Patrick Henry reportedly declared, "Give me liberty, or give me death!" he assumed that liberty was something reserved for whites. A slaveholder himself, Henry admitted that slavery was morally problematic, but "Henry's understanding of the discrepancy between his words and his deeds never led him to act differently," notes sociologist James Loewen. "I am drawn along by the general inconvenience of living here without them," Henry explained.[1]

In every generation, people have found rationales for systems of social and legal inequality. Native Americans had no rights in the new country, so their land could be taken for white settlement. Africans had no rights, so it was all right to enslave them. Women had no rights, and their labor was generally unpaid. Contract workers had few rights, and their labor was underpaid. Immigrants, as well as workers in other countries, have also been deprived of rights—yet their low-paid labor provides the cheap products that our economy depends on.

Today, a large and growing portion of our population lives without the full rights of citizenship. Noncitizens work, pay taxes, go to school, and raise families; they live in our cities and towns; they participate in religious, sports, and community events; they serve (in disproportionately large numbers) in the military. But both the law and popular opinion deem them somehow different from the rest of us, and not eligible for the rights and privileges that 90 percent of the population enjoys.

As of March 2005, more than 35 million people, a little over 10 percent of the total U.S. population, were foreign born. Most of these people had legal permission to be here, but about a third of them did not. About one-third of all foreign-born people (documented and undocumented) came from Mexico, the largest source of immigrants. Over half came from Latin America and the Caribbean as a whole (including Mexico). Another 18 percent came from East Asia. The top ten sending countries were Mexico (10.8 million); China (1.8 million); the Philippines (1.5 million); India (1.4 million); El Salvador (1.1 million); Vietnam (996,000); Cuba (948,000); the Dominican Republic (695,000); Canada (674,000); and Korea (672,000).[2]

During the 1990s the number of immigrants increased rapidly. In 1990, only 19.8 million reported foreign birth. In 2000, the figure was 31.1 million.[3] (These figures do not include the 3.4 million Puerto Ricans who lived in the continental United States according to the 2000 census. They are U.S. citizens, although they are also Latin Americans.) Although one wouldn't guess it from the increasing anti-immigrant agitation in the 2000s, immigration actually slowed significantly after the end of the 1990s.[4] Nativism, or anti-immigrant racism, responded as much to other trends in society as to the actual number of immigrants coming in.

The current influx of immigrants is often compared to the last large and sustained wave, which occurred between 1860 and 1920, when the rate of foreign-born persons in the population ranged from 13 to 15 percent. Because the total population was smaller, this higher percentage represented a smaller number of people. Prior to the 1980s, the highest year for the foreign born was 1930, when 14.2 million people reported foreign birth. Most of these immigrants came from southern and eastern Europe.[5]

During the 1860–1920 immigration wave as well as during that of the late twentieth century, immigration was accompanied by nativist reactions. Nativists worried that immigrants would fail to assimilate, would undermine the perceived linguistic, cultural, and racial homogeneity of the country, would take American jobs, and would lower wages. Commentators in various forums warned that the newcomers would bring disease and crime. Today, Arthur Schlesinger worries about the "disuniting of America," while Samuel Huntington fears the "challenges to American national identity."[6] They seem to be echoing the California attorney general who wrote in 1930 that "only we, the white people, found [America] first and we want to be protected in our enjoyment of it."[7]

While there are many parallels between the two waves of immigration, there are also some significant differences. Ideas about race have changed significantly over the course of the century. In the nineteenth century overt racism was widely acceptable in the mainstream; today it is not. By the late nineteenth century, the academy sought to provide biological and scientific research proving the existence and nature of racial difference. Scholars of all stripes dedicated themselves to classifying the globe's population according to their supposed racial characteristics. Europeans were divided into the "Anglo-Saxon race," the "Slavic race," the "Mediterranean race," and many others. Popular and legal thought varied as to whether the latter belonged to the "white" race or not.

The relationship of race to nationality has shifted in slippery ways, and is in fact still in flux. Ideas about race in the United States have been shaped by immigration, and have also shaped the way people think about immigration. Every U.S. census has used different categories to identify race. Until 1930 Mexicans were "white," then the 1930 census designated "Mexican" as a separate race. Today, most people inside the academy and outside agree that race and ideas about racial difference are social constructs rather than scientific facts. Even the census itself acknowledges that racial categories "are sociopolitical constructs and should not be interpreted as being scientific or anthropological in nature."[8]

The U.S. economy has changed drastically between the two periods of immigration. In the 1890s, the United States was industrializing rapidly, and most new immigrants went to work in the mines, mills, and factories of the new industrial economy. In the 1960s, the country was undergoing deindustrialization, and the mines, mills, and factories were closing, creating a "rust belt" in the very regions that had previously been a magnet for immigrants. The deindustrialized economy still created a demand for immigrant workers, but in the service industry: "cleaning—all kinds of cleaning," as one immigrant worker, who ran his own small house-cleaning business, described it to me. Immigrants now clean houses and office buildings. They clean hospitals and restaurants. They clean people, clothes, and cars.

The new wave of immigrants was also different because they came from countries in Latin America and Asia that had a history of U.S. interventions and political and economic domination. In this respect, postindustrial immigration to the United States was not unique. European countries were experiencing the same phenomenon. Industrialization had been accompanied, everywhere that it occurred in the late nineteenth century, by colonial expansion—military, political, and economic. (Sometimes this expansion took the form of direct colonial rule; sometimes it consisted of informal means of control.) Deindustrialization, in the late twentieth century, was accompanied by immigration from former colonies. These different events were part of an interconnected historical process, and to understand the differences between the two waves of immigration, we need to understand the entire historical process.

These issues of race and the global economy were also interrelated. People who were colonized were considered racially different in ways that left very deep roots in the modern world, and colonialism also left long-term economic consequences. When people of color from the colonies migrated to Europe and the United States in the late twentieth century, these deep racial and economic colonial roots were coming to the surface.

Many societies have struggled with the question of what makes a person eligible for rights. Does everybody have rights, simply by virtue of being human? Or are rights restricted to a select group of people in a society, who are defined as "citizens"? And if rights are dependent on citizenship, how is it decided who is a citizen?

After World War II there was a widespread repudiation of the kind of legalized discrimination that many believed led to the horrors of Nazism. The Universal Declaration of Human Rights, passed by the United Nations General Assembly in 1948, upheld the idea that there was no justification for governments excluding certain groups of people from rights. The Declaration asserts in Article 2 that "Everyone is entitled to all the rights and freedoms set forth in this Declaration, without distinction of any kind, such as race, color, sex, language, religion, political or other opinion, national or social origin, property, birth or other status," and in Article 6 that "Everyone has the right to recognition everywhere as a person before the law."[9] The declaration is unambiguous: rights apply to *all* people.

The Universal Declaration embodies an expansive notion of rights. In addition to many of the rights protected by the U.S. Constitution and Bill of Rights, the Universal Declaration defines and guarantees social and economic rights like the right to work, the right to equal pay, and the right to education, food, housing, and medical care.

The U.S. Constitution is a bit more ambiguous about what rights belong to all people and what rights belong only to citizens. The law has always been utilized to exclude some people from rights—often to the advantage of employers, who can then exploit those who are excluded. When we look at the past, we generally decry exclusionist ideas and laws. (The Nuremberg Laws, for instance, excluded Jews from rights in Germany.) There is no real logic to excluding people from rights based on immigration or citizenship status. Citizenship was based on race during most of the history of the United States and has historically been employed as a way to justify discrimination.

The U.S. Department of Homeland Security provides a "civics lesson" to help those people who are eligible for citizenship prepare for the test they'll have to take as part of the process. One question reads "Whose rights are guaranteed by the Constitution and the Bill of Rights?" The answer is unequivocal: "All people living in the United States." The lesson goes on to elaborate:

> One reason that millions of immigrants have come to America is this guarantee of rights. The 5th Amendment guarantees everyone in the United States equal protection under the law. This is true no matter what color your skin is, what language you speak, or what religion you practice. The 14th Amendment, ratified after the Civil War, expanded this guarantee of rights. No state would be able to abridge, or block, the rights of any of its citizens.[10]

The reality is a bit more complex. United States law has always been, and still is, restrictive about who deserves rights. Until the Civil War, federal statutes took for granted, and upheld the notion, that citizenship and rights should be based on race, and that rights depended upon citizenship, which was reserved for white people. The distinction was not between the native born and immigrants, as it is today, but rather between whites—who were citizens—and nonwhites, who were not. The Fourteenth Amendment, passed in 1868, for the first time extended citizenship to "all persons" born in the United States—except Native Americans:

> All persons born or naturalized in the United States and subject to the jurisdiction thereof, are citizens of the United States and of the State wherein they reside. No State shall make or enforce any law which shall abridge the privileges or immunities of citizens of the United States; nor shall any State deprive any person of life, liberty, or property, without due process of law; nor deny to any person within its jurisdiction the equal protection of the laws.

The Amendment thus expanded citizenship by partially separating it from race for the first time. Before this, citizenship was restricted to whites, and rights were restricted to citizens. But citizenship was not completely separated from race yet. First, the "subject to the jurisdiction thereof" clause excluded Native Americans, even those born in U.S. territories. Second, anybody *born* in the United States was automatically a citizen—but only white people could be *naturalized* as citizens. The 1870 Naturalization Act extended the right to naturalize to Africans and people of African descent—but they were not the only non-"white" people in the United States.

Citizenship was particularly denied to Asians—by 1882 they were prevented from coming to the United States at all, in part to ensure that nobody of Asian descent would gain citizenship by virtue of being born here. Chinese people were not permitted to naturalize until 1943. Even then, they were subject to an immigration quota of 100 per year. Filipinos and (Asian) Indians were granted the right to become citizens in 1946, and the "Asiatic barred zone" established in 1917 was finally abolished in 1952. It was not until 1965, however, that the 100-per-year quotas were lifted for Asian countries.

The Fourteenth Amendment's second sentence extends rights even more broadly than the first: no *person*—apparently, citizen *or* noncitizen—can be denied equal protection under the law. The apparent contradiction in the Amendment left it up to the courts to rule on what it meant in specific cases. The U.S. Supreme Court has given contradictory rulings. Two important decisions argued that citizenship status could not be used to deprive people of rights. In 1971, *Graham v. Richardson* prohibited states from discriminating against legal immigrants in granting welfare benefits; in 1982, *Plyler v. Doe* ruled that all children have a right to public school education regardless of legal status. Other decisions, though, allowed states to discriminate, and the 1996 welfare reform incorporated unambiguous discrimination against legal immigrants.[11]

Most Americans assume that voting rights and citizenship are identical, and that restricting voting rights to citizens is natural and reasonable. But even this relationship is far from clear-cut. "For a good part of our country's history," explains political scientist Ron Hayduk, "voting rights were determined not by citizenship, but by whether or not one was a white, male property holder. Thus, women and post-emancipation blacks—who were considered citizens—could be denied voting rights. In fact, alien suffrage . . . actually buttressed the privileging of propertied, white, male Christians."[12]

The Constitution allows states and municipalities to determine voting criteria. Until the 1920s, many of them permitted noncitizens to vote. It was in the context of particular political struggles—and large-scale immigration after 1850—that states began to exclude noncitizen immigrants from voting.

Hayduk explains:

> In the Civil War era, Southern states resented immigrants' opposition to slavery. In many states, wartime hysteria and the Red Scare after World War I made Americans want immigrants to "prove" their loyalty before receiving the privilege of voting. And in others—like Texas during the women's suffrage struggle—ending the immigrant vote was a way for political status quo supporters to counteract the broadened electorate that came with the 14th Amendment (voting rights for African-American men) and 19th Amendment (voting rights for women).[13]

Restrictions on immigrants' voting rights went along with other restrictions—"literacy tests, poll taxes, felony disenfranchisement laws, and restrictive residency and voter registration requirements—all of which combined to disenfranchise millions of voters."[14]

Many European countries, and even municipalities in the United States, allow noncitizen voting as a matter of course. Noncitizens live in communities, they pay taxes and use services—why should they be excluded from political participation in the place where they live? Conversely, some citizens are denied voting rights. In most states citizens who have been convicted of a felony cannot vote. Residents of Washington, D.C., could not vote in presidential elections until 1964, and Puerto Rican residents still can't. And citizens who live in these two areas have no congressional representation.

An analysis of the 2000 census showed that in eighty-five California cities, over 25 percent of the adult population is disenfranchised because they are not citizens. In twelve of these cities, noncitizens are over 50 percent of the adult population. "A substantial number of persons, who contribute to our economy and our government's revenues, are being denied political representation," explains the general counsel for the Mexican American Legal Defense Fund.[15]

If the Fourteenth Amendment is taken literally, then it is routinely violated in the United States today. Noncitizens are openly denied *equal* protection, and some of them—those who are undocumented—are denied *any* protection under the law. Their very existence is termed "illegal." In many ways, their situation is comparable to that of African Americans prior to the 1870s, and again after the 1890s when Reconstruction's attempts to make citizenship real for African Americans were unraveled. Undocumented persons, and even legal immigrants, may be physically present in the United States, but they are not treated equally under the law.

Just as in every period of U.S. history, the law today discriminates by excluding large sectors of U.S. society from its protection, and from the concept of equal rights. Rather than race, ethnicity, or gender—which have been discredited as reasons for excluding portions of the population from access to citizenship—today the dividing line is generally place of birth. Unlike in the past, there is no blanket prohibition on citizenship for any group of people. Nevertheless, many people in the United States are denied the right to become citizens, and denied the rights that go along with citizenship.

Just as it seemed obvious to those in power in the past that race, ethnicity, and gender were legitimate reasons to exclude portions of the population from rights, many American citizens today believe passionately in the need to divide the population between citizens and noncitizens, and immigrants between those deemed "legal" and those deemed "illegal." That those classed as the latter categories should be denied rights, and that large groups of people should be denied the right to become citizens or to become "legal," is considered self-evident.

Although the exclusion itself is rarely questioned, resentment against immigrants and attempts to further marginalize them are rampant in today's society. The suggestion that noncitizens, too, are created equal is virtually absent from the public sphere. However, claims that immigrants take American jobs, are a drain on the American economy, contribute to poverty and inequality, destroy the social fabric, challenge American identity, and contribute to a host of social ills by their very existence are openly discussed and debated at all levels of U.S. society.

In a series of short chapters, this book seeks to dismantle the myths that inform the major debates about immigration in today's United States. To address issues ranging from "America is a nation of immigrants" to "immigrants take American jobs," it draws on immigration history, critical race studies, labor history, Latino and Asian studies, analyses of globalization, and other academic areas to show how the parameters and presumptions of today's debate distort the way we think about immigration.

Each chapter seeks to identify and challenge the assumptions that underlie some of the prevailing arguments about immigration. The book challenges the way we understand U.S. economic and immigration history. I argue that since before this country was founded, its economy has been global. The prosperity of some within our borders has always depended on the cheap labor of others from both inside and outside our borders. This cheap labor has been justified and guaranteed by excluding certain workers from the categories of people who are afforded rights. Although race is seldom directly invoked in anti-immigrant discourse today,

I argue that race is so deeply tied to ideas about citizenship and immigration that it is central to the discussion. I conclude with an attempt to imagine what a humane immigration policy would look like, and how creating a humane immigration policy would connect to other changes at a national and global level.

PART ONE

IMMIGRANTS AND THE ECONOMY

Some of the most widespread myths about immigration have to do with its effects on the economy. Immigrants are blamed for causing or exacerbating a wide variety of economic ills, from unemployment to low wages to the underfunding of government services. It's undeniable that many Americans feel economically pinched and vulnerable, and that the numbers of Americans in this situation are increasing. But what role does immigration really play in the larger picture of the U.S.—and the global—economy?

MYTH 1

IMMIGRANTS TAKE AMERICAN JOBS

"Immigrants take American jobs" is one of the most common arguments brandished to justify the need for a restrictive immigration policy. There are two main fallacies in the argument. They are fallacies that serve a purpose. In the pages that follow I will explain the two fallacies, and explain why, although they are so problematic, so many of us nonetheless believe them.

The first fallacy lies in the very concept of "American" jobs. In fact, today's economy is so globally integrated that the idea of jobs having a national identity is practically useless. In many industries, employers seek to reduce costs by employing the poorest, most vulnerable people. They do this by moving to parts of the world where poverty and inequality create a vulnerable labor force, and by supporting policies that create poverty and inequality at home—including immigration policies that keep immigrants coming, and keep them vulnerable. So we'll look at what the concept of "American jobs" really means.

The second fallacy is closely tied to the first: the notion that immigration and immigrants reduce the number of jobs available to people already in the United States. In fact, immigration plays a much more complex role in the employment picture, and many different factors affect employment and unemployment rates.

Most analyses point to two major structural developments in the U.S. economy as the main causes of the shifting employment pattern in the late twentieth century: deregulation and deindustrialization. Deregulation of major sectors of the economy and cutbacks in federal social spending under the presidencies of Ronald Reagan and his successors went hand in hand with a rise in plant closures and outsourcing.

Not only did jobs disappear in this period, but the nature of jobs in this country underwent a shift. High-paying manufacturing and government jobs evaporated, and many of the new jobs that were created were low-paying jobs in the service sector, at places like McDonald's and Wal-Mart. Again, this is part of a larger structural change in the U.S. economy and the way it is integrated into the global economy. Immigration makes up just a very small part of this bigger picture.

Generally, businesses seek to keep their expenses as low as possible, to achieve the greatest profit margin possible. One way of doing this is by moving workers, and moving production, around the globe. In the early days of the industrial revolution, factories brought workers to the point of production. Some came from local rural areas to the new industrial cities, while in the United States some came from halfway across the globe.

In today's economy—sometimes called the "postindustrial" economy—it's been industries as well as workers that have relocated. The global economic restructuring since World War II has created what some have called a "new international division of labor."[1] Low-paid workers in the Global South used to produce and export raw materials, which fueled the industrial revolution in the north. The cheap raw materials produced by these workers—with great profits for investors—contributed to the prosperity of the United States and Europe, which was based partly on the artificially low prices made possible by their labor.

In the postwar restructuring, the industries started to move to the south to take advantage of the low wages there. People in the south still produced items for export to the north—but now they exported manufactured goods as well as raw materials.

The New England textile industry was one of the first to experiment with plant relocation, shifting its production to the U.S. southeast starting at the very beginning of the twentieth century in search of lower costs. By the end of the century, the trend had spread to almost all industries.

Just as the U.S. working class began to share fully in the benefits of industrialization in the mid-twentieth century, U.S. businesses increased their search for cheaper workers abroad. As early as the 1940s, the U.S. government was collaborating with businesses on ways to re-create the low-wage, high-profit system that was being undermined inside the United States by the rights achieved by factory workers. Their first experiment was in Puerto Rico. Dubbed "Operation Bootstrap," it offered incentives to U.S. businesses to transfer the most labor-intensive portions of their operations to the island. The island government offered land, loans, buildings, and infrastructure to companies willing to take the risk.

The Puerto Rican program was so successful—for businesses—that it was soon extended to Mexico. The U.S. and Mexican governments turned once more to A.D. Little, a consulting firm in Cambridge, Massachusetts, that had helped set up Puerto Rico's Operation Bootstrap, to design a similar program for Mexico. The Border Industrialization Program went into operation in 1965.

It was an ingenious move. Since it was getting harder and harder to deprive workers of rights inside the United States because of popular mobilizations, unions, and laws protecting workers and their right to organize, companies found it more and more attractive to move the jobs across the border, to where U.S. laws did not apply. It worked so well that by the 1970s the U.S. government was extending this strategy to the Caribbean, and later on to Central and South America and Asia. The North American Free Trade Agreement, or NAFTA, which went into effect in 1994, pushed it even further. U.S. manufacturing industries began a wholesale move abroad in search of the country that would offer them the lowest wages, the most docile (or nonexistent) unions, and the least regulation of their activities.

Workers in countries like Mexico, El Salvador, and the Dominican Republic have seen a flood of foreign investment in offshore production—often called *maquiladora* production, referring to the system whereby companies outsource the most labor-intensive part of the production process. Workers in these countries gain in some ways when Nike, Liz Claiborne, or Dell opens a factory there. They gain because jobs are created; but they also lose because the new jobs are dependent on employers' keeping wages, benefits, and government regulation low. If workers, or governments, start to demand a greater share of the profits, the company can simply close down and move to a cheaper location.

This phenomenon creates what some analysts have termed the "race to the bottom." Workers and governments compete with each other to offer businesses lower taxes, lower wages, and a more "business-friendly environment" in order to attract or preserve scarce jobs. The competition may be more devastating in already poor Third World countries, but it's going on in the United States as well, as communities pour resources into schemes to attract businesses.[2]

By maintaining and exploiting global inequalities, the U.S. economic system has managed to create a high-profit/cheap-product model. But it is unsustainable, both morally and practically. In practical terms, we saw the results in the 1930s: if workers aren't paid enough to be consumers, there will be no market and production will crash. The New Deal tried to remedy this by restructuring the division of resources and putting more money into the hands of the working class. Industry responded by accelerating its move abroad. But the high-profit, low-wage system is no more sustainable globally than it was domestically.

As for the second fallacy—that the number of people determines the number of jobs—at first glance, it might seem logical: there is a finite number of jobs, so the more people there are, the more competition there will be for those jobs. By this theory, periods of population growth would also see rising unemployment rates, while periods of population decline would see falling unemployment. How can it be, then, that a recent study by the Pew Hispanic Foundation of employment patterns throughout the United States over the past decade found that "no consistent pattern emerges to show that native-born workers suffered or benefited from increased numbers of foreign-born workers"?[3]

Clearly, the relationship between population size and the number of jobs available is not quite as simple as it might seem. In fact the number of jobs is *not* finite, it is elastic, and affected by many factors. Population growth creates jobs at the same time that it provides more people to fill jobs, and population decline decreases the number of jobs at the same time as it provides fewer people to work at them. Population growth creates jobs because people consume as well as produce: they buy things, they go to movies, they send their children to school, they build houses, they fill their cars with gasoline, they go to the dentist, they buy food at stores and restaurants. When the population declines, stores, schools, and hospitals close, and jobs are lost. This pattern has been seen over and over again in the United States: growing communities mean more jobs.

The number of people in a given community is not the only thing that affects the number of jobs, though. Some people work in jobs that directly service the local community, and those jobs are directly affected by population growth or decline. But many jobs produce goods and services that are consumed elsewhere. Automobile plants in Detroit, or fruit farms in California, or garment factories in El Salvador, or call centers in Bangalore, depend on global, not local, markets.

As has become painfully obvious in recent decades, businesses that service a global market don't generally have a strong commitment to the local community. A factory may provide jobs in Detroit for a decade, or a century, and then close and move elsewhere for reasons that have nothing to do with the size of the population in Detroit. In fact population loss often follows job loss—when a factory closes, people, especially younger workers, leave a community because they lose their jobs—and then local businesses also start to close, because the population can't support them anymore.

Pretty much all of us live, work, and consume in both a local and a global economy. The local economy may be more visible, but we eat grapes grown in Chile, drive cars assembled in Mexico, and pump them with gas from Kuwait or Colombia. And people in the United States produce goods and services that are sold abroad. The United States imports and exports over $100 billion worth of goods and services every month.[4] So jobs in the United States have a lot to do with the global economy, not just what's happening locally.

Between 1920 and the 1970s, the unemployment rate in the United States generally hovered between 4 percent and 6 percent. The exception was the Depression in the 1930s (a period of very low immigration), when unemployment skyrocketed to over 20 percent. The rate dropped again by the 1940s with the Second World War. Starting in the late 1970s it rose, peaking at almost 10 percent in the early 1980s, and remained between 5 percent and 8 percent for the rest of the twentieth century and into the twenty-first.[5] Many factors have influenced the fluctuations in the unemployment rate over the years. Immigration rates, though, do not appear to have any direct relationship at all with unemployment rates.

During the period from the 1870s to the 1910s there was a very high rate of immigration into the United States. World War I, and restrictive immigration legislation in 1917, 1921, and 1924, cut way back on the number of arrivals. The Depression of the 1930s, with its devastating rates of unemployment, occurred when hardly any immigrants were coming into the country. The deportation of thousands of people of Mexican origin from the Southwest during the decade did little to affect employment rates in that region (unless you count those employed to carry out the deportations). Unemployment during the Depression, like unemployment today, simply had very little to do with immigration.

MYTH 2

IMMIGRANTS COMPETE WITH LOW-SKILLED WORKERS AND DRIVE DOWN WAGES

Wages in the United States have indeed been falling with respect to prices, and with respect to profits, since the 1960s. In 2006, wages and salaries made up a smaller proportion of the country's gross national product than at any time since the government started collecting those statistics in the 1940s, while corporate profits rose to record highs.[1] The gradual gains made by the working class during the first half of the twentieth century were being chipped away in the second half—just as immigration rates began to rise again. Why did this happen?

If you look only at the small picture, it indeed seems to be the case that immigrants and low-skilled citizens are competing for the same jobs. Businesses certainly *want* this kind of competition—it means they can find people willing to work for low wages. And, businesses argue, low wages keep prices low.

It's true, if you look at the U.S. economy as a whole, that prices for some kinds of products have gone down and that people in the United States are consuming a lot more of those products. Clothing and electronics are two good examples of how manufacturers and retailers have been able to use low wages and deregulation—both inside the United States and outside—to keep prices down. And U.S. consumers are buying lots of those things. Most of the clothes and electronic devices we buy are produced outside of the United States in factories that pay low wages, in places where governments keep taxes and other expenses low. So companies can keep prices low for consumers while still making a profit.

If prices for some consumer products, especially those produced abroad, are kept low, prices for other kinds of goods and services are rising in today's economy. A lot of the things that are getting more expensive are basic human needs—things like health care, housing, and education. Middle-class and even low-wage workers in the United States may benefit from cheap shoes, cell phones, and iPods, but at the same time they are finding it harder and harder to buy a house, get the health care they need, or send their kids to college.[2]

What's going on? And what does it have to do with immigration?

Study after study has shown that since the late 1970s, the distribution of wealth in the United States has become more and more skewed. By the end of the century the richest 1 percent of the population owned about 30 percent of the country's wealth, and the top 5 percent controlled 60 percent of the wealth.[3]

True, immigration also increased during the last decades of the century. But this does not prove that immigration was the cause of the growing inequality. Coincidence does not prove cause and effect. Rather, the same global economic restructuring that exacerbated inequality in the United States *also* contributed to increasing immigration. In fact, we could argue that cause and effect are reversed: increasing inequality *created demand for immigrant workers* and thus spurred immigration.

Rising inequality, concentration of wealth, and cheap products all go together. To understand how and why immigration fits into the global economy, we need to understand how this system works.

Products can be produced cheaply when business expenses—things like wages, benefits, taxes, infrastructure costs, and the cost of complying with health, safety, and environmental regulations—are low. Businesses have always wanted to keep their costs down—that's why they tend to oppose regulations such as those listed above, which add to their expenses. Inequality helps them keep costs down in several ways.

First, when workers are poor and lack legal protections, they are more willing to work long hours for low wages. So businesses benefit when there exists a pool of workers without economic or legal recourse. This is one of the reasons why early industries relied on immigrant workers; why agriculture in the United States has used slavery, guest workers, and immigrants; and why businesses tend to oppose restrictions on immigration today. It also helps to explain why deregulation of the economy, and even why increasing repression and criminalization of immigrants, actually creates greater demand for immigrant workers.

In a democracy, it's hard to justify deliberately keeping part of the population poor and excluded by legal means. Racial slavery was one means used to do precisely that until the 1860s. Temporary guest-worker programs, Jim Crow laws, and other forms of legalized discrimination—in the North as well as the South—were other methods that kept a supply of workers without rights available until the 1960s. In the western United States, legal restrictions against U.S. citizens of Mexican origin served the same purpose as Jim Crow did in the South. It's no coincidence that in periods when rights have been expanded to previously excluded sectors of the population, businesses have sought new sources of exploitable labor.

Sociologists have used the concept of the *dual labor market* to explain how this system has worked throughout the history of the United States (and other industrialized countries). The *primary labor market* refers to jobs that are regulated. Workers are protected by laws that establish living wages, health and safety standards, and benefits. Their jobs are long term and secure. Their right to organize unions is accepted and protected by law.

The *secondary labor market* consists of jobs that are generally not regulated. Wages are low, and working conditions are dangerous and often harmful to workers' health. Not only are the jobs unpleasant and poorly compensated, they are also dead end: there is little or no room for advancement.

Poor working conditions are often justified with subtle or overt prejudice against the people who work in those jobs: they are seen as less intelligent, less deserving, and congenitally suited for the kind of work they do. Often they are not citizens. Until the 1930s, most factory work fell into this category.

Why would people acquiesce to working under these substandard conditions? Inequality helps to provide the answer, in some obvious and some less obvious ways.

Let's look at the obvious ways first. Inequality maintains a population of poor people who lack access to resources, and who may have little alternative but to accept jobs under the worst of conditions.

But inequality works on a regional and global, as well as a local, level. These larger inequalities help to explain why industrial societies have tended to rely on *immigrants*, rather than the domestic poor, to fill jobs in the secondary sector.

The southern and eastern European immigrants who filled the factories and the mines and the Latin American and Asian immigrants who now fill the sweatshops, the fields, and the lower ends of the service sector share several characteristics that are related to regional inequalities.

First, *the dollar is worth more in the home country than it is in the United States.* Immigrants tend to believe that the United States is a country of fantastic wealth, where hard work can bring unbelievable reward. And they're right: 26.3 percent of Mexicans, 46.4 percent of Filipinos, and 90.8 percent of Nigerians live on two dollars or less per day in their respective homelands.[4] These people know that they could earn more in the United States.

Of course, the cost of living in Mexico, the Philippines, and Nigeria is much lower than the cost of living in the United States. The minimum wage, or subminimum wage, that a Mexican worker might earn in the United States wouldn't be enough to support a family here—but it can mean the difference between utter dispossession and dignified survival, or between minimal survival and hope for the future, in Mexico, Nigeria, or the Philippines.

This brings us to the second piece of the puzzle: *immigrants are willing to accept conditions abroad that they would never accept at home.* Many people immigrate planning to spend a brief period of time working abroad, living under the most onerous conditions, and earning money that can be used to help those who remain at home, and then to return home themselves to purchase a house, buy land, or start a business. Migrant workers who come with this intention are not terribly concerned about their living conditions while in the United States—they are often willing to work fifteen hours a day, live six to a room, forgo any social life, and eat out of tin cans in order to save as much money as possible and return home as quickly as possible.

Immigrants do jobs that American citizens wouldn't do—in Mexican president Vicente Fox's notorious words, "jobs that not even blacks want to do"—because they are not trying to live a decent life in the United States.[5] They couldn't, on their meager wages. Their frame of reference is their much poorer home country, and what seem like unlivably low wages here are worth a lot more there.[6]

Over time, however, even these migrants' frame of reference changes. Some do return home with their savings, but others begin to set down roots in their new land and bring or establish families here. World War I, and the subsequent immigration restrictions, accelerated this process for European immigrants, who could no longer return home. As they begin to assimilate into the new society, immigrants are no longer willing to work for substandard wages and conditions. They begin to struggle to better their conditions in their new home.

For the European immigrants in the early part of the century, this process was in general successful. The growing strength of labor unions, combined with federal legislation that began to regulate the conditions of work, changed the conditions of factory work during the 1930s and 1940s. Instead of being dangerous and underpaid, the assembly line became the basis of a middle-class lifestyle. Industrial workers could buy houses and cars, take vacations, and send their children to college.

Some sectors of the economy were excluded from the New Deal reforms of the 1930s and 40s, though, and remained in the secondary labor market. The main areas left out of the reforms were agriculture and domestic service. (As of 2006 the National Labor Relations Act *still* excludes agricultural and domestic workers.) Since these were the sectors where most of the workers were and are people of color, especially African Americans and Mexican Americans, most analyses conclude that the New Deal reforms, while not explicitly mentioning race or privileging white people, in fact had the result (and probably the goal) of reinforcing racial inequality and the dual labor market.

Other federal reforms of the middle of the century also contributed to hardening preexisting racial inequalities. The GI bill of 1944, for example, helped millions of people from the working class get access to higher education—but most colleges and universities in the United States still excluded blacks. Federal housing loans and mortgage policies also exacerbated racial inequality, since racial covenants, written and unwritten local codes, and lending policies clearly excluded nonwhites.

When southern and eastern European immigrants came to the United States in the late nineteenth and early twentieth centuries, they were not considered white—at least not fully white. They went to work in the factories and in the mines under abominable conditions. Because they were poor, because they were marginalized as noncitizens and as newcomers, and because legislation protecting the rights of factory workers was in its infancy, businesses were able to use them as a secondary labor market to build their industries. African Americans and Mexican Americans were even further legally marginalized because racial segregation and discrimination were widespread and encoded in the law.

The mid-century reforms extended rights to European immigrants at the same time as they drew the lines more firmly against people of color, whether immigrants or citizens. People of Mexican origin—including many who were U.S. citizens—were deported in massive waves in the 1930s, just as the New Deal was beginning to improve the conditions of work in the factories. The continuous expansion of rights described in the introduction needs to be qualified with the continuous exclusion from rights that accompanied it. Each period of expansion and reform has been accompanied and/or followed by a redefinition of exclusion. And exclusion guaranteed the continuing existence of a pool of workers for the secondary labor market.

The *bracero* program established in 1942 created a new legal way for Mexican workers to be used as a secondary labor market. They were brought into the country on temporary visas that defined them as "arms" rather than people (bracero comes from the Spanish word *brazo*, or arm) and treated essentially as indentured servants of the businesses that hired them. In the northeast, a similar recruitment program brought Puerto Ricans—who, like African Americans, were citizens, but second-class citizens—to work in the farms and fields.

In the 1960s, the formal system of racial segregation in the United States was dismantled, and a new wave of government programs ranging from affirmative action to food stamps tried to redress the results of centuries of legally enforced racial inequality and exclusion. The Voting Rights Act, moreover, acknowledged that blacks had been excluded by administrative means from full citizenship. The bracero program was also tacitly acknowledged to be a violation of people's rights. According to a former U.S. commissioner of immigration, "its failings could no longer be reconciled with civil rights-era sensibilities about how people should be treated in a democratic society."[7]

There was a difference, though, between African Americans, who were slowly, tortuously, accorded the rights of citizenship, and immigrants. For some immigrants, rights also slowly expanded, and opportunities for citizenship opened. Explicit racial exclusion of blacks from citizenship was dismantled through a series of steps beginning with the Fourteenth Amendment in 1868 and continuing through the Voting Rights Act in 1965. Along the way, the racial barriers to Asian citizenship were dismantled as well, on a slightly different schedule.

But the imposition of numerical quotas on Mexico and other Western Hemisphere countries for the first time, also in 1965, led to a huge rise in the numbers of "illegal immigrants" who did not have access to this expansion of rights. And the new wave of globalization of labor, begun by Operation Bootstrap in Puerto Rico in the 1940s and 50s and expanded with the Border Industrialization Program in Mexico in 1965, created new mechanisms for corporations to have access to workers who were excluded from democratic rights. Both of these U.S.-designed programs created privileged industrial export zones and invited U.S. factories to relocate in them.

But people of color who were citizens were still subject to social barriers, and people of color who were immigrants faced new structures, like the national quotas still in place today, that shut them out. Many new post-1965 immigrants from Latin America and Asia were as definitively excluded from citizenship, or from the rights of citizenship, as previous generations of people of color had been. The category of immigrants classed as "illegal" mushroomed because of the way the law was designed, and because of the increasing economic demand for immigrant workers.

The 1965 law dismantled the national origins quotas, which were by then universally seen as discriminatory. In their place, it created a uniform quota system of 20,000 per country for the Eastern Hemisphere, and a 150,000 ceiling for the Western Hemisphere—that is, Canada, the Caribbean, and Latin America. (This was changed in 1976 to implement the 20,000-per-country quota for Western Hemisphere countries as well.) Preference went to family members of people already in the United States.

The family preference system reinforced the phenomenon of chain migration from poor countries. It was based on the humanitarian idea of family reunification, but its implications went far beyond that. It meant that immigration became structured by circles of relationships with individuals in the United States. It meant that countries with strong recent histories of immigration, like Mexico, quickly overflowed their quotas, because lots of Mexicans had family members in the United States and could take advantage of the priority given to close relatives of people (legally) in the United States. In contrast, countries without a large presence, like Paraguay, scarcely filled their quotas.

The uniform quota system also embodied its own forms of discrimination. Huge countries like China and India had the same quota as tiny countries—so a would-be immigrant from, say, Oman, had a much higher chance of receiving a visa than one from a more populous country. And different sets of historical factors (which will be discussed below) meant that the "demand" for visas in some countries was very low, while in others it was very high. So some countries never reached their limits, meaning that it was very easy for their citizens to obtain visas.

For other countries, there were far more than 20,000 applicants. This meant that if you didn't fall into a preference category, that is, if you didn't have family members in the United States or particular job skills, your chances of getting a visa were virtually nil. Even for people with close relatives who were citizens or permanent residents of the United States, the wait could be years or even decades.

One problem at the root of the new quota system is that it dealt with countries, rather than with people. At the same time that it claimed to end discrimination based on national origin, it still made national origin the decisive factor in determining whether an individual could receive permission to come to the United States or not. By treating all countries equally, it treated *people* unequally. A person's chances of getting permission to come to the United States no longer depended on his or her race—now it depended on how large his or her country of origin was, and on how many others in that country wanted to come.

Furthermore, the 1965 law ignored the long-standing economic integration, and in particular the labor migration, between Mexico and the United States. Migrant networks and systems that had roots even older than the bracero program didn't disappear when the program ended, and the jobs Mexican migrants had filled, mostly in seasonal agricultural work, didn't vanish either. Because it placed such a low cap on Mexico at the same time that the bracero program ended, the law vastly increased the numbers of "illegal" migrants. Abolishing the bracero program without creating any other legal mechanism to allow Mexicans to work in the United States turned people who had formerly worked legally into "illegal immigrants." One hundred years after slavery was ended, continuing legal distinctions among people ensured that secondary labor market employers would have an ample supply of workers—workers who could not turn to the law to protect their rights in the workplace.

The structures of exclusion were compounded by the global inequalities that made immigrants, as people who had a dual frame of reference (the home country and the United States), more likely to accept, rather than challenge, their exclusion.

Domestic reforms of the 1960s may have extended full legal citizenship to African Americans, but structural inequalities, and the secondary labor market, persisted. By the 1970s an economic assault on the poor of all races began to unravel the social safety network established in the previous decades. And the connection of rights to *citizenship* was reinforced. Growing numbers of Latin American and Asian immigrants created a new pool of noncitizens who could be treated as workers without rights.

The unraveling of the social safety network, combined

with deindustrialization, severely undermined the primary sector of the labor market. But as the primary labor force was contracting the secondary labor force was expanding. As women entered the workforce in larger numbers and people had to work longer hours to support a middle-class lifestyle, many of the services connected to the *reproduction* of the labor force moved out of the home and into the private sector. Fast food, child care, elder care, and home health care became rapid-growth sectors. These were jobs that could not be moved abroad. But if workers without social and economic rights might be recruited, they could provide a low-wage labor force.

Economist Nancy Folbre calls this aspect of the economy the "invisible heart"—as opposed to the "invisible hand" that classical economists argue governs the marketplace. The paid world of work and business, she explains, couldn't exist without the unpaid, invisible network of care provided mostly by women. The economic shifts that began in the 1970s both demanded more working hours outside the home and cut back on public services and benefits, creating what Barbara Ehrenreich and Arlie Hochschild have termed a "care deficit" in the first world.[8] Much of the new wave of immigrants that began after 1965 moved in to fill this care deficit.

The changing economy created other secondary-sector jobs too. New systems of subcontracting enabled some jobs to slip from the regulated to the unregulated sector. Factories threatened to close unless unionized workers gave up their gains of the past fifty years to compete with low-cost workers abroad. U.S. cities tried to woo in industries by offering them exemptions from the regulations and taxes that had been part of the redistributive model of the mid-twentieth century. So conditions in the primary sector of the workforce deteriorated at the same time that jobs were being lost to outsourcing.

Some of these changes chipped away at the social and economic rights that workers had attained through decades of struggle and legislation. Prisons and security also became growing employers as larger portions of the population were pushed into economic hopelessness.

There were some moves that stripped African Americans of political rights, too. Criminalization of drug use and draconian sentencing laws and patterns contributed to the astonishing statistic that in 2003 nearly one-fourth of African American men in their thirties had prison records—while only slightly over 10 percent had college degrees.[9] Over five million Americans are legally disenfranchised because of felony convictions, including 13 percent of African American men.[10] While still technically citizens, they are deprived of one of the essential rights of citizenship in the United States: the right to vote. (Other U.S. citizens also have restricted voting rights: Puerto Ricans on the island can't vote in presidential elections and have no representation in Congress; citizens living in Washington D.C. could not vote in presidential elections until 1964, and still have no representation in Congress.)

Immigrants, however, have no political rights to begin with. If we frame our discussion by talking about countries and nationalities, it may seem logical that people should have rights only in the country where they are citizens. But if we frame the discussion by talking about workers and their rights, we see a different pattern. For centuries, the United States and other industrialized countries have institutionalized inequalities by granting rights to some people but not to others. People without rights may be slaves, they may be colonial subjects, they may be racial and ethnic minorities, or they may be immigrants, or they may be people in or subject to another country. In all cases, though, governments have made sure that there are people without rights to fulfill business's need for cheap workers and high profits. When one group of workers has gained rights, historically, businesses—with government help—have simply looked elsewhere to define or create a new group of rightless workers.

Exclusionary citizenship has allowed the United States to maintain a fiction of equal rights while also making sure that employers have access to workers without rights. From the very founding of the country, the idea that "all men are created equal" coexisted with the fact of slavery, and the exclusion of large numbers of people physically present in the United States from the rights of citizenship. This contradiction continues to characterize U.S. law and society: many people who are physically present here are still excluded from the rights and privileges of citizenship. Keeping some people outside of the bounds of equality and citizenship served employers' need for cheap labor in the past, and continues to do so today.

So let's return to the original question: do immigrants

compete with low-skilled workers for low-paying jobs? Yes. But the *reason* that this competition exists is because *too many people are deprived of rights.* The proposals for immigration reform that are circulating today do nothing to expand the rights of those currently excluded—in fact they do just the opposite. Further restrictions on immigration will not lower the numbers of immigrants—as long as the demand for labor is there, history has shown that immigrants will keep coming. And further restrictions will only compound the problem of immigrants' lack of rights. The answer to the low-wage problem is not to restrict the rights of people at the bottom even more (through deportations, criminalizations, etc.) but to challenge the accord between business and government that promotes the low-wage, high-profit model.

When historians look at the evolution of workers' rights in the United States, they often point out that the institution of slavery, and the subsequent dispossession and disenfranchisement of African Americans there, put the South far behind the North in the growth of labor organizing and the gains in workers' rights. White workers in the South may have clung to their status of legal and racial superiority, but in fact the entrenched racial inequalities undermined the socioeconomic status of poor whites as well. It is hard to organize unions when there are lots of even poorer people eager for your job, and it's hard to organize for social justice when you're focused on preserving your slight advantage over those below you.

It's important to understand, though, that it wasn't the

presence of African Americans—or the fact that they were African American—that made it hard for poor whites to bring about social change. It was the institutions of slavery and racial exclusion, the *disenfranchisement* and *dispossession* of African Americans, combined with white racism, that prevented poor southern whites—as well as blacks—from achieving social justice and equality. Likewise, it is not the *presence* of immigrants that lowers the wages and living standards of citizens—it is the fact that immigrants are deprived of rights, combined with anti-immigrant racism, that creates the obstacles to improving the lives of poor people.

Decisions and policies made by governments and by corporations are the main factors that determine wage levels. Global—and local—inequalities allow economies to sustain a low-wage, secondary-sector labor market. Both immigrants and poor people in general, inside and outside the deindustrializing countries like the United States, are the common victims of the lavish lifestyles of the wealthy and the profits of corporations.

If we look back at history, the greatest challenges to the low-wage, high-profit model have come through federal legislation and social movements, including labor organizing. When governments offer businesses freedom from regulation and deprive workers of rights, low wages and high profits flourish, and democracy suffers. Whether the excuse is race, or economic status, or nationality, a portion of the U.S. population has always been disenfranchised. Business may benefit from this system, but the population as a whole does not. Expanding democratic rights downward benefits everyone, especially those at the lower end. The contradiction between the rights of immigrants and the rights of citizens who are poor is more apparent than real.

MYTH 3

UNIONS OPPOSE IMMIGRATION BECAUSE IT HARMS THE WORKING CLASS

Unions in the United States have not always opposed immigration. But the mainstream union movement in the United States in the twentieth century did—until the 1990s. The reasons had to do with how the U.S. union movement came to define its goals and its place in U.S. society.

At the beginning of the twentieth century, the American Federation of Labor (AFL) competed with other, more radical unions. The Industrial Workers of the World (IWW) promoted a social justice agenda and tried to organize the most dispossessed workers. It sought profound social and economic change. The AFL, in contrast, basically accepted the social order. It concentrated mainly on trying to organize and improve the conditions of the most skilled workers—creating what some have called an "aristocracy of labor." By the middle of the century, with the growth of the Congress of Industrial Organizations (CIO) and its later unification with the AFL, this evolved into the creation of a "private welfare state" for union workers.[1]

While some of its European counterparts sought a larger

public agenda of improving conditions for the working class, the AFL-CIO concentrated on improving conditions for union members. Rather than fighting to raise the minimum wage or create a national health-care system, the AFL-CIO sought to improve benefits for organized workers through their contracts with their employers. The privileged position of (mostly white) union workers actually depended on the existence of the dual labor market—domestically and globally—that produced goods and services cheaply. That is, some get low wages so that others can enjoy cheap products.

The IWW rejected the way citizenship was used in the United States to deprive some workers of their rights. At its founding convention in 1905, "Big Bill" Haywood began his remarks by explaining, "I turned over in my mind how I should open the convention. I recalled that during the French Commune the workers had addressed each other as 'fellow citizens,' but here there were many workers who were not citizens so that would not do . . . I opened the convention with 'fellow workers.' "[2]

Contrast this to the stance taken by Samuel Gompers, the president of the AFL, in the same year. "Caucasians," he announced proudly, "are not going to let their standard of living be destroyed by Negroes, Chinamen, Japs, or any others."[3] As David Roediger explained, "They opposed entry of 'the scum' from 'the least civilized countries of Europe' and 'the replacing of the independent and intelligent coal miners of Pennsylvania by the Huns and Slavs.' They wrote of fearing that an 'American' miner in Pennsylvania could thrive only if he 'latinizes' his name. They explicitly asked . . . 'How much more [new] immigration can this country absorb and retain its homogeneity?' "[4]

The United Mine Workers of America argued that labor unions needed to uphold "Caucasian ideals of civilization" and used its journal to warn continually against the "yellow peril."[5]

Gompers became an anti-imperialist in the case of the Philippines, not because of any solidarity with the Philippine independence movement or opposition to colonial expansion, but because of racism. "We do not oppose the development of our industry, the expansion of our commerce, nor the development of our power and influence which the United States may exert upon the destinies of the nations of the earth," he explained. The problem was the "semi-savage population" of the islands—he did not want to see it incorporated into the United States.[6]

"If the Philippines are annexed," he demanded, "what is to prevent the Chinese, the Negritos and the Malays coming to our country? How can we prevent the Chinese coolies from going to the Philippines and from there swarm into the United States and engulf our people and our civilization? . . . Can we hope to close the flood-gates of immigration from the hordes of Chinese and the semi-savage races coming from what will then be part of our own country?"[7]

As Vernon Briggs shows, "At every juncture, and with no exception prior to the 1980s, the union movement either directly instigated or strongly supported every legislative initiative enacted by Congress to restrict immigration and to enforce its policy provisions."[8] Until 1917, those immigration restrictions were purely race based, forbidding first Chinese, then Japanese, then all Asian immigration.

Over the course of the first decades of the twentieth century, though, the AFL, gradually and grudgingly, began to accept the new European immigrant workers into its fold. "Although self-interested, wary, and incomplete, the AFL opening to new immigrant workers initiated a process that could transform 'semiracial' typing of already arrived new immigrants . . . Although specifically defending (and equating) 'white' and 'American' standards of wages, consumption, and working conditions, the more hopeful came to regard it as possible that some new immigrants could be taught those standards."[9] Workers who could not be encompassed within this new definition of whiteness, however, were still excluded.

Southern and eastern European workers established themselves as white, as Irish workers had before them, by embracing rather than challenging the racial hierarchy. The Irish "learned to distinguish themselves in racial struggles and to establish their claim as 'whites.' They did so by taking up arms for the white Republic against the blacks in the Philadelphia race riots and the New York draft riots of 1863. They also took part in the anti-Chinese movement in California."[10] Michael Rogin argues that first the Irish, then southern and eastern European immigrants, established their claim to whiteness through adopting white racism, specifically through the use of blackface: "Blackface . . . distanced the Irish from the people they parodied. Demonstrating their mastery of the cultural stereotype, Irish minstrels crossed the cultural border. . . Blackface brought Irish immigrants into the white working class, freeing them from their guilt by black association."[11]

The Democratic Party opened itself to Irish immigrant workers on a pro-slavery platform before the Civil War, to "counterbalance the numerical advantage of the Northern free states and maintain slavery by the assimilation of the Irish into the white race."[12] The party became "a coalition of urban machine constituents and southern Negrophobes."[13]

Union policies like "father-son" clauses in the building trades and apprenticeship and seniority systems helped to maintain racial exclusivity in the AFL and later AFL-CIO well into the 1960s.[14] The federation opposed the NAACP's attempt to have domestic and agricultural workers included under the Wagner Act in 1935.[15] It worried that the 1964 Civil Rights Act would challenge its history of discrimination and fought to have past discrimination exempted from the Act's purview.[16]

The exclusionary system worked fairly well for many white workers until the restructurings of the 1970s began. But in the 1970s the New Deal social compact began to fall apart. Businesses accelerated their shift abroad, and government began to dismantle the New Deal social welfare state. It took the AFL-CIO until 1993 to come to terms with the fact that the old system was unrecoverable—and that its survival depended upon reaching out to immigrant workers. At its 1993 convention the federation adopted a resolution criticizing those who "exploit public anxiety by making immigrants and refugees the scapegoats for economic and social problems." "Immigrants are not the cause of our nation's problems," the resolution stated. It affirmed the rights of immigrants, whether documented or undocumented, and encouraged unions "to develop programs to address the special needs of immigrant members and potential members" and collaborate with "immigrant advocacy groups and service organizations."[17]

The "New Voices" leadership that took over the federation in 1995 continued the trend away from exclusiveness and the "private welfare state." The new leadership categorically rejected the idea "that immigrants are to blame for the deteriorating living standards of America's low-wage workers." Rather than focusing on immigrants as the problem, it proposed "increasing the minimum wage, adopting universal health care, and enacting labor law reform as the remedies for the widening income disparity in the nation."[18]

MYTH 4

IMMIGRANTS DON'T PAY TAXES

Immigrants, no matter what their status, pay the same taxes that citizens do—sales taxes, real estate taxes (if they rent or own a home), gasoline taxes. Some immigrants work in the informal economy and are paid under the table in cash, so they don't have federal and state income taxes, or social security taxes, deducted from their paychecks. So do some citizens. In fact every time the kid next door babysits, or shovels the snow, he or she is working in the informal economy.

Much of the service sector operates in the informal sphere. Nanny jobs and housecleaning jobs—which tend to be held primarily by women—generally use informal arrangements whether the workers are citizen or immigrant, documented or undocumented. But increasingly, jobs that used to be in the formal sector—like factory jobs—have sunk into the informal sector through elaborate systems of subcontracting. Textile and apparel manufacturing are particularly notorious in this regard.[1]

There are some benefits for employers, and for consumers, from this informal sector. Employers can pay lower wages than those required by law. Consumers receive access to cheap products and services provided by these low-wage, untaxed workers.

But workers in the informal economy don't fare so well. They don't have access to any of the worker protections that come with formal employment, like minimum wage or health and safety regulations. Workers in the informal economy can't get unemployment insurance or workers' compensation and generally get no benefits from their employer (like health insurance or sick leave or vacation time).

It's hard to calculate exact numbers for the informal economy because, by definition, it's unregulated. One recent study in Los Angeles estimated that immigrants made up 40 percent of the city's population, and one-fourth of these were undocumented. The informal economy accounted for some 15 percent of the city's workforce, and undocumented workers were concentrated there: 60 percent of workers in the informal economy were undocumented.[2]

Many immigrants work in the formal economy, in which case they have all of the same tax deductions from their paychecks as citizens do. Undocumented immigrants who work in the formal economy generally do so by presenting false social security numbers. The Social Security Administration estimates that about three-fourth of undocumented workers do this.[3]

Public commentary about this practice is often quite angry. In fact, though, the only ones who lose anything when workers use a false social security number are the workers themselves. Taxes are deducted from their paychecks—but if they are undocumented, they still have no access to the benefits they are paying for, like social security or unemployment benefits.

Even with a false social security number, the federal and state taxes that are deducted from a worker's paycheck will go into federal and state coffers. Social security payments are either credited to whoever's number was used, or, if a worker uses a number that doesn't belong to anybody, they go into the Social Security Administration's "earnings suspense file." As of 2005, Social Security was receiving about $7 billion a year through false social security numbers—allowing it to break even, because that's about the same amount as the difference between what it paid out in benefits and what it received in payroll taxes. According to the *New York Times*, "illegal immigrant workers in the United States are now providing the system with a subsidy of as much as $7 billion a year."[4] Yet these workers will never be able to receive Social Security benefits.

MYTH 5

IMMIGRANTS ARE A DRAIN ON THE ECONOMY

This is a complicated question that requires us to define "the economy." Generally, those who say immigrants are a drain on the economy are referring to the myth that immigrants use more in public services than they pay in taxes. In fact the majority of immigrants, being of prime working age and ineligible for many public services, tend to contribute more to the public sector than they actually use. However, many of the services they do tap into are local services (schools, transportation, libraries), and the new wave of immigration coincides with federal cutbacks to these services, placing a greater burden on local governments. (The native born, it should be said, *also* tend to use more in local services than they pay in local taxes.)

Several state-level studies have tried to assess the level of state and federal taxes that immigrants, documented and undocumented, pay compared to the level of state and federal services that they receive. Early studies in California and in the Southwest as a whole and more recent studies in the Southeast, which is seeing the highest rates of immigrant population growth now, have come to similar conclusions. Immigrants, documented and undocumented, are more likely to pay taxes than they are to use public services. Undocumented immigrants aren't eligible for most public services and live in fear of revealing themselves to any government authorities. Documented immigrants are eligible for some services—but even they hesitate to use them, since they fear that being seen as a public charge will make it harder for them to stay, apply for citizenship, or bring family members. Nationally, one study estimates that households headed by undocumented immigrants use less than half the amount of federal services that households headed by documented immigrants or citizens make use of.[1]

There are some government services that both documented and undocumented immigrants do benefit from: public schools, emergency medical care, and the public safety system (e.g., police, prisons). These are known as "mandated services," which federal authority requires state government to provide to all people, regardless of immigration status.

The only kind of public service that immigrant households use at higher rates than natives is food assistance programs such as food stamps, WIC, and free or reduced-cost school lunches. However, it's not the immigrants themselves who use this aid—they're usually not eligible—but rather their U.S.-born children, who are citizens.[2]

The Georgia Budget and Policy Institute estimates that undocumented immigrants in the state pay between $1,800 and $2,400 a year in state and local taxes, including sales, property, and income taxes (for those who file W-2 forms with false social security numbers). This brings from $200 to $250 million into state and local budgets.

"Do undocumented immigrants pay enough in taxes to cover the services used?" the report asks.

> For undocumented immigrants, the answer is unclear. However, for legal immigrants, studies have shown that first-generation immigrants pay more in federal taxes than they receive in federal benefits. The same does not hold true for state taxes and services, however, as first-generation immigrants often use more in services than they pay in taxes. However, the descendants of the first-generation immigrant correct that pattern and contribute more in taxes at both the federal and state level than they consume in services at both levels. Each generation successively contributes a greater share due to increased wages, language skills, and education.[3]

Similarly, in Colorado undocumented immigrants were found to pay about $1,850 in state and local taxes if they were working on the books, and $1,350 (in sales and property taxes) if they were working under the table. Thus the estimated 250,000 undocumented immigrants in that state were paying $150 to $200 million in state and local taxes, covering about 70 to 85 percent of the approximately $225 million they used in state and local services.[4]

If immigrants don't make heavy use of social services and they do pay taxes, then why don't their taxes cover all of, or more than, the services they do use? Mostly because they earn such low wages that their tax payments are lower than those of people who earn higher wages. Low wages mean that less is withheld for income taxes, and it means that they have less money to spend, so they pay less in sales and property taxes than people who earn more. In fact, our progressive system of income taxes is designed to take a greater chunk of the income of a high earner than a low earner. So if immigrants are paying less, it's because they're earning less.

A Florida study found similar results: new immigrants tend to have lower levels of education and lower earnings—and thus pay less in taxes—than the U.S. population as a whole. Within fifteen years, immigrants' earnings—and their taxes—have caught up.[5]

Since the 1990s, economists have started to use a more complex model for evaluating the effects of immigration with respect to taxes and public services. Instead of just looking at the cost of educating the children of immigrants, for example, they also look at the potential future tax revenues of those children. This approach, called "generational accounting," is based on the notion that when government spending exceeds tax revenues—that is, when the government operates at a deficit, as is currently the case—future generations essentially have to pay back the debt. So the numbers of new immigrants in future generations will affect how the costs of the debt are distributed—more immigrants means less burden on the native born.[6]

From the perspective of businesses, employing immigrant workers, and workers in other countries, brings some special advantages. Again, a comparison to slavery is enlightening. Slaveholders generally preferred to purchase slaves of prime working age and strength. They discovered that it was cheaper to continually import new slaves and overwork them to death rather than having to pay for the *reproduction* of their slave labor force. Brazilian slaveholders found that they could recover the cost of purchasing a slave with two years of harsh labor, so that any amount of time that a slave survived after that was pure profit. The average was three more years—and the profit could then be used to buy a new slave worker.

When the slave trade was abolished—at the beginning of the nineteenth century in the United States, much later in the century in Brazil and Cuba—slaveholders had to shift their strategies. In order to maintain a slave population, they had to foster reproduction. This meant that they had to invest more in their existing slaves. They had to provide for children who were too young to work, and for the women or elders who cared for the children. They had to increase the level of subsistence so that slaves would *not* die within five years.

Immigration and outsourcing (moving production abroad) fulfill the same logic, from the perspective of businesses. The New Deal social compact put the burden on businesses to give back to their workers, and to society, in order to support the reproduction of the labor force. Wages, benefits, and taxes were all ways in which businesses contributed to social reproduction.

If businesses could find a new source of workers that was

reproduced outside of the United States and the New Deal social compact, however, they could save money. If a worker is born and raised in Mexico, works for a U.S. enterprise (either in Mexico or in the United States) between the ages of twenty and forty, then returns to the home community, it is the Mexican family, community, and institutions that bear the costs of reproduction. The U.S. company gets just what the slaveholder got: workers in their prime working years, with no investment in the society that raised them or that will care for them as they age.

Of course some immigrants, even if they originally intended to work for a short time and return home, end up staying. Over time, they lose those special immigrant qualities that make them willing to work for low wages in substandard conditions. In other words, they become more like citizens: they need to work for wages, and in conditions, that will sustain their life here. The opportunities for upward mobility that European immigrants enjoyed may no longer exist, but immigrants do shift in the kinds of jobs they will do, the kinds of conditions they will accept—and the amount of taxes that they pay.

As workers leave the secondary sector—whether because they return home, grow older, or set down roots here—employers remain avid for new immigrants to replace them. A significant exception to the model of economic improvement over time is undocumented immigrants. Unlike "legal" immigrants (refugees, legal permanent residents, and those who become naturalized citizens), whose incomes increase significantly in proportion to their time in the United

States, undocumented immigrants tend to remain on the margins of the U.S. economy. Even those who had been in the United States for ten years or more in 2003 had a family income of only $29,900—as compared to natives, whose family incomes averaged $45,900, refugees at $45,200, legal permanent residents at $44,600, and naturalized citizens at $56,500.[7]

It's not surprising, then, that 39 percent of undocumented immigrant children live below the poverty line, and 53 percent lack health insurance.[8] The results of the 1986 Immigration Reform and Control Act, which granted amnesty to a significant portion of the undocumented population then in the United States, are also clear. Once they achieved legal status, migrants were able to improve their levels of education and income.[9] By maintaining arbitrary status differences and excluding millions of people from legal rights, and by ensuring that immigrants will continue to arrive, and that some will continue to be classed as "illegal," U.S. policies guarantee the existence of a permanent underclass.

MYTH 6

IMMIGRANTS SEND MOST OF WHAT THEY EARN OUT OF THE COUNTRY IN THE FORM OF REMITTANCES

Remittances are a very important part of the global economy. They often account for a larger portion of poor countries' income than foreign aid does. ("Remittances" refers to money that immigrants send home to family members in the home community.) In 2004, immigrants from Latin America sent over $30 billion to their home countries—in 2005, over $50 billion.[1]

In 2004, 10 million Latin American immigrants—some 60 percent of the Latin Americans living in the United States—sent home remittances, usually ranging from $1,000 to $2,500 a year, or 10 percent of their annual income. (The total income of Latin American immigrants in the United States is $450 billion.) Although only 10 percent of what an average immigrant earns here, the money sent home represents from 50 percent to 80 percent of the household income for those at home in Latin America.[2] Ninety percent of immigrants' wages are spent in this country. Citizens, too, of course, spend some of their earnings abroad—directly, if they travel, or indirectly, if they purchase imported goods.

Because of the complex nature of the global economy, it's very hard to untangle exactly who benefits from every dollar spent. For example, if you buy a cup of coffee at Starbucks, you're paying for rent on the building, workers' wages, baristas' wages, maintenance workers' wages, managers' salaries, and utilities (and everything that goes into producing the utilities, including perhaps the importation of coal, oil, or gas), plus various forms of insurance, advertising, the furniture, the music, the mugs, and the many people involved in the production, processing, trading, and shipping of coffee, not to mention the shareholders in all of these different enterprises, and the executive officers and their retirement packages . . .

How remittances are spent is also very complex. A significant—though shrinking—portion goes to the institutions that process the financial transactions. In the 1990s the cost of sending money to Latin America was almost 20 percent of the amount sent, though this declined to slightly under 10 percent after 2000.[3] Still, local banks and transfer companies, all of which employ people, are one beneficiary.

Some portion of the remittances goes directly to family members and is spent on food, health care, clothing, home improvement, and education. This kind of spending can have both local and global effects, since many of the products and materials used in these areas are imported. When the money is spent locally, it can also help to improve the local economy.

In some ways, remittance money is more efficient than foreign aid at improving people's lives in ways that reduce migration. Foreign aid often comes with strings attached. Sometimes it has to be spent on products, or machinery, made in the country that gives the aid. Sometimes it has to be spent on "development" projects that actually make the lives of the poor worse—like a dam, or a mine, that displaces people from their homes, or like subsidized corn that floods markets and bankrupts poor farmers.

Some remittance money goes to hometown associations that are involved in different types of development projects like building schools, water systems, or sports facilities. (In Spanish these are sometimes called *organizaciones de pueblo, clubes de oriundos,* or *clubes sociales comunitarios.*) The Mexican government has been particularly active in using incentives to channel money into economic development. In perhaps the consummate irony, the state government of Guanajuato has implemented a program of joint ventures with hometown associations to develop garment maquiladora factories in migrants' home communities. These factories produce clothing for foreign companies that in turn export to the United States. As of 2000, six of these factories had been established, with plans in the works for sixty more.[4] Other studies have shown that U.S. companies choose Guanajuato as a site for building factories because, with such a large proportion of families relying on remittances, they are able to pay lower wages there than in other parts of Mexico.[5]

Remittances can have other contradictory effects too. In

El Salvador, one study found that a significant portion of remittances is spent on imported consumer goods. Imports rose from 27.7 percent of El Salvador's GDP in 1990 to 42 percent in 2004. So rather than creating jobs, the system creates new incentives to migrate, since only families who count migrants among their members can afford this kind of consumption.[6]

Remittances, then, are one element in an extremely integrated global economy. If we look only at the flow of remittances, it looks like a lot of money is leaving wealthy countries and going into poor countries. But if we look at the global economy as a system, remittances are just one small piece of a very complex, multidirectional flow.

PART TWO
IMMIGRANTS AND THE LAW

The U.S. Declaration of Independence asserts that humans are endowed with "unalienable rights," and that if a government deprives them of such rights, "it is the right of the people to alter or to abolish it." Henry David Thoreau cautioned against "undue respect for law" and urged his readers to rely instead on conscience. He decried the "thousands who are *in opinion* opposed to slavery and to the war, who yet in effect do nothing to put an end to them." "When a sixth of the population of a nation which has undertaken to be the refuge of liberty are slaves, and a whole country is unjustly overrun and conquered by a foreign army, and subjected to military law, I think that it is not too soon for honest men to rebel and revolutionize," he declared in *Civil Disobedience.* (He was referring to the U.S. invasion of Mexico in 1846.)[1]

In his "Letter from a Birmingham Jail," Martin Luther King too insisted that laws be judged from the standpoint of conscience and morality. "A law is unjust," he wrote, "if it is inflicted on a minority that, as a result of being denied the right to vote, had no part in enacting or devising the law." He was talking, of course, about laws enforcing segregation made by southern legislatures for which blacks were denied the right to vote. He could just as well have been talking about laws that discriminate against immigrants, a minority in a country that denies them the right to vote.

(Some have even argued that all the world's citizens should be allowed to vote in U.S. elections, given the degree of U.S. political, military, and economic power around the globe. "Every action of the US President affects my life deeply in political, economic, social and cultural terms," wrote Indian journalist Satya Sagar in 2004, in an only partly facetious essay explaining why U.S. elections should be opened to all.)[2]

Much of the current anti-immigrant agitation stems from the idea of the sanctity of the law, and abhorrence of the crime that immigrants commit when they violate immigration law. This section will examine the arbitrary and discriminatory nature of immigration law and argue that the legal categories it creates have historically been informed by racism and politics, rather than humanitarianism, justice, or the idea that all men (or all people) are created equal.

MYTH 7

THE RULES APPLY TO EVERYONE, SO NEW IMMIGRANTS NEED TO FOLLOW THEM JUST AS IMMIGRANTS IN THE PAST DID

One of the most oft-repeated—and most puzzling—comments regarding the debate on immigration goes something like this: "I'm not against immigration, but I'm against illegal immigration. New immigrants should play by the rules, like our parents and forebears did."

The sentiment reveals a lot about how we've been taught to think about U.S. history: we've been taught to think of this as a country of white, voluntary immigrants. The history of people who don't fall into that category is incidental, rather than central, to the story we learn in school. "The rules," though, were different for Europeans than for Africans, Asians, and Native Americans. For the latter, "the rules" meant enslavement, exclusion, and conquest.

What the people (generally of European origin) who point to "the rules" ignore, moreover, is that when *their* parents and grandparents came to the United States, they in fact did exactly what so-called "illegal" immigrants are doing today. They decided to make the journey, and they made it.

All they had to do was get together the boat fare. The rules were different then. U.S. law explicitly limited citizenship and naturalization to white people. Nonwhites, however, were denied both entry and citizenship. Through a complex process of omission and commission, the law dictated open immigration for white people and restricted immigration for people of color. Immigration and naturalization law created, in the words of Aristide Zolberg, "a nation by design."[1]

Between 1880 and World War I, about 25 million Europeans immigrated to the United States. They did not have visas or passports. A very small number of them—about 1 percent—were turned back at Ellis Island because they were deemed to be criminals, prostitutes, diseased, anarchists, or paupers.[2] There were no illegal immigrants from Europe because there was no law making immigration illegal for Europeans.

It wasn't until 1924 that numerical restrictions were placed on white European immigration, creating a situation in some ways similar to today's, in which would-be immigrants had to compete, before they left home, for the few available visas to come to the United States. The restrictions placed on Europeans, though, pale in the face of those that the 1924 legislation placed on non-Europeans: as "aliens ineligible to citizenship" because they belonged to the "colored races," they were excluded altogether. Although the 1924 quotas did not apply to the Western Hemisphere—Congress couldn't figure out what "race" Mexicans actually belonged to—the legislation also invented the concept of the "illegal immigrant" and created the Border Patrol to keep

Mexicans out. (I describe these restrictions in more detail in the section on immigration and race below.)

The last major immigration reform, in 1965, finally removed the racially defined quota system, and replaced it with a uniform quota system for all countries. But the new laws of 1965 were only one factor leading to the huge increase in immigration from Latin America and Asia.

Even more important has been the acceleration of what we now call "globalization." Today's globalization builds on structures developed during the centuries of colonialism that preceded it. One aspect of globalization in the second half of the twentieth century has been a huge population movement from the former colonies into the lands of their former colonial masters. In order to comprehend this global phenomenon, we have to look at the socioeconomic and cultural legacy of colonialism.

In broad strokes, the European colonialism that shaped the modern world could be described as the conquest of people of color by white people, the massive transfer of natural resources out of the colonies and into the colonial powers, and the dispossession of formerly self-sufficient native inhabitants as their lands were taken for the export economy. Modern colonialism began with Spanish and Portuguese expansion in the 1400s, followed by northern European expansion in the 1600s and 1700s. By the end of the 1800s the European countries had carved up much of Africa and Asia, while the United States was extending direct and indirect rule into the newly independent countries of Latin America.

Formerly self-sufficient natives of these lands conveniently served as a cheap or coerced labor force to exploit the resources (land, minerals). The colonial powers received the raw materials and agricultural products that allowed them to industrialize; the colonies were left with depleted lands and political structures that were geared toward tyranny and exploitation. If the dispossessed masses rebelled, colonial armies were quickly mobilized to repress them.

Consider the example of the Dominican Republic. It was colonized first by Spain, then by the United States. (The U.S. invaded and occupied the Dominican Republic from 1916 to 1924 and again in 1965.) The first U.S. occupation brought about massive dispossession and transfer of Dominican land into the hands of U.S.-owned sugar plantations; the second brought about the modern version of colonialism (sometimes called "neocolonialism"), in which the governments of poor countries are forced to create low-wage, low-tax, low-regulation environments for the benefit of U.S. corporations. (The proliferation of these export-processing zones there explains why so many of our clothes bear tags saying "Made in the Dominican Republic.")

The United States has the highest standard of living in the world, and it maintains it by using its laws, and its military, to enforce the extraction of resources and labor from its modern version of colonies, with little compensation for the populations. It is no wonder that people from these countries want to follow their resources to the place where they are being enjoyed.

Most of today's immigrants come from countries where

the United States has been deeply involved in the past hundred years: in addition to the Dominican Republic, they come from such countries as Mexico, the Philippines, El Salvador, Guatemala, Vietnam, and Cambodia. Given the numerical quotas and the preference system that privileges family members of those already in the United States, for most would-be immigrants from the Third World (i.e., people from former colonies—i.e., people of color) there is literally no way at all to receive permission to come here. Even immediate family members, who are granted priority, have to wait up to twenty years to get permission. For those without family members who are citizens or permanent residents, the current law is little different from the one passed in 1924: it permanently excludes them.

The law, then, is inherently discriminatory. It primarily benefits close relatives of U.S. citizens and of permanent residents. For most people who want to come to the United States, the law simply forbids it.

When the law prevented blacks from sitting at a lunch counter reserved for whites, black people protested the law by breaking it—sitting down where they were told they weren't allowed. On many occasions in the past, people have struggled for equality before the law by committing civil disobedience and entering an institution, a neighborhood, a city, a state, or a country that forbids their presence. Today, we think of many of those who broke the law in the past in the interest of equal rights as heroes.

MYTH 8

THE COUNTRY IS BEING OVERRUN BY ILLEGAL IMMIGRANTS

According to the United Nations High Commission on Human Rights, "the expression 'illegal migrant' should not be used. It contradicts the spirit and violates directly the words of the Universal Declaration of Human Rights which clearly states in Article 6 that 'Everyone has the right to recognition everywhere as a person before the law.' The preferred term is 'undocumented migrant.' "[1] Some immigration scholars prefer "unauthorized migrant," since many of the people who fall into this category do in fact have documents, but not *valid* documents—they may be false, or expired, or otherwise fail to authorize their presence.[2]

The difference between "legal" and unauthorized, undocumented, or "illegal" immigrants is nowhere near as clear-cut as most people imagine. Some people who enter the country legally will become illegal if they overstay their visa; some people who enter illegally or become illegal are actually in the process of legalizing their status, especially if they have a close relative who can sponsor them.

Many families and households include people of differing immigration status: citizens by birth, naturalized citizens, legal permanent residents, people on immigrant visas, and undocumented immigrants.

A 2004 study by the Pew Hispanic Center, based on the 2000 census and the 2004 Current Population Survey, found 35.7 million foreign-born residents in the United States; in 2005 this was up to 37 million. Of these, 11.3 million (11.5 million in 2005) were naturalized citizens; 10.4 million (10.5 million in 2005) were legal permanent residents; 10.3 million (11.1 million in 2005) were unauthorized migrants; 2.5 million (2.6 million in 2005) were refugees; and 1.2 million (1.3 million in 2005) were temporary legal residents (holding a nonimmigrant visa like a tourist or a student visa).[3] As of early 2006, estimates had risen to between 11 and 12 million unauthorized migrants.[4]

Of the unauthorized migrants, over half—5.9 million (6.2 million in 2005)—were from Mexico, and another 2.5 million from elsewhere in Latin America. The rest came from Asia (1 million in 2004; 1.5 million in 2005), Europe and Canada (600,000 in both 2004 and 2005), and Africa (400,000 in both years).[5]

Hard information on these unauthorized migrants is hard to come by. But the Pew report argues that most of those who came from Mexico entered "without inspection"—that is, they crossed the border without valid entry documents—while most of those from outside the Americas entered with valid visas but overstayed them. For the rest of Latin America, migrants are assumed to be divided between the two categories—some crossing the border without documents, and some overstaying valid visas.[6] The California Rural Legal Assistance Foundation estimates that half of all unauthorized migrants are EWIs—people who "entered without inspection," that is, crossed the border without passing through a border control post. The other half are visa overstayers—people who entered with a valid visa but did not depart when the visa expired.[7]

In addition, something like 1 to 1.5 million of the unauthorized migrants have "quasi-legal" status in the United States. They may have requested asylum, or begun the process of acquiring legal permanent resident status, or become eligible for a new category of authorized presence, like the temporary protected status offered to Salvadorans and Nicaraguans.[8]

The stereotype most Americans hold of the "illegal immigrant" is a single, adult male, here to work temporarily. Indeed some of the unauthorized migrant population falls into this category. Of the approximately 11.1 million unauthorized migrants in the country as of March 2005, only about 25 percent (2.4 million) were single men, fewer than 10 percent (730,000) were single women, and 16 percent (1.8 million) of unauthorized migrants were children under eighteen. The remaining 3.9 million women and 5.4 million men lived in families, whose members varied in terms of immigration status. In particular, they included three million children who were U.S. citizens.[9]

Overall, unauthorized migrants tend to have lower levels of education and work at lower-paying jobs than do authorized migrants or citizens. They are especially overrepresented in agriculture and construction work—some of the most unregulated sectors of the labor market.[10] Only 4.3 percent of all workers in the United States are unauthorized migrants, but they constitute 19 percent of workers in agriculture, 17 percent in cleaning and building maintenance, 12 percent in construction, 11 percent in food preparation, and 8 percent in production.[11]

In industrial work, unauthorized workers are particularly present in food manufacturing and in textiles and apparel manufacturing. These two industries offer good examples of how global economic restructuring has affected the U.S. labor market.

Textiles and garments were two of the first industries to experiment with the mobility of capital. The U.S. textile industry began in New England in the mid-nineteenth century. Before the century ended, textile magnates were looking to invest in places where they could produce more cheaply. South Carolina, Alabama, Georgia, and other places in the U.S. south offered low taxes, cheap labor, official repression of unions, and subsidies to entice capital.

Factory owners in the north played a double game during the early to mid-twentieth century. They invested in the south, taking advantage of the incentives southern communities offered. Then they told their northern workers that they were being undercut by southern competition and would have to lower wages and speed up the work pace in order to remain competitive. Often they ran their northern factories into the ground before closing them permanently.

In the second half of the century, the game turned global.

Manufacturers opened plants in Puerto Rico, in Mexico, and elsewhere in Latin America and in Asia. They imposed cost-cutting measures in their U.S. plants, claiming "foreign" competition. When they had reduced conditions in their U.S. factories to make them competitive with the Third World, they began to import Latin American workers —claiming that no U.S. workers wanted the jobs. New England's oldest textile towns, like Lowell, Massachusetts, and Central Falls, Rhode Island, turned into new immigrant centers in the 1960s, '70s, and '80s, as textile employers recruited workers in Puerto Rico and Colombia.[12]

Meatpacking followed a somewhat different trajectory. While the textile industry was able to use the threat of plant relocation to successfully undermine union organizing attempts or to keep unions weak, the meatpacking industry became one of the bastions of industrial union organizing in the 1930s, which succeeded in significantly improving the conditions of workers. "From the 1930s to the 1970s," explains Lance Compa, "meatpacking workers' pay and conditions improved. Master contracts covering the industry raised wages and safety standards. In the 1960s and 1970s, meatpacking workers' pay and conditions approximated those of auto, steel, and other industrial laborers who worked hard in their plants and through their unions to attain steady jobs with good wages and benefits. Meatpackers' wages remained substantially higher than the average manufacturing sector wage."[13]

In the 1980s, meatpackers began an assault on the conditions of their unionized workers. Management's response to the 1985 strike at a Hormel meatpacking plant in Austin, Minnesota, epitomized the industry's commitment to breaking and eliminating unions in their plants. The strike lasted for over a year and a half, and garnered national attention from labor activists and others who hoped to stem the tide of concessionary bargaining. The cautious national union (UFCW) opposed the militant local, and the strike was crushed. It was the beginning of the dismantling of the unionized meatpacking sector.

Because it is perishable, meat is harder to transport than many of the items whose production was moved abroad in the 1980s. Rather, the meat industry replicated what the agricultural industry had been doing since the nineteenth century: it began to "bring in the Third World." As Compa explains it, "Instead of exporting production to developing countries for low labor costs, lax health, safety and environmental enforcement, and vulnerable, exploited workers, U.S. meat and poultry companies essentially are reproducing developing country employment conditions here."[14]

MYTH 9

THE UNITED STATES HAS A GENEROUS REFUGEE POLICY

Since World War II, U.S. law has provided for certain would-be immigrants to be granted special rights as refugees. Despite the folklore (repeated in the citizenship exam) that "the Pilgrims came to America to gain religious freedom"[1] and the Statue of Liberty inscription welcoming "your tired, your poor, your huddled masses yearning to breathe free," prior to World War II the country in fact had no immigration provisions at all for refugees. Although the admission of refugees since then is often thought of as a humanitarian policy, its character has been much more political than humanitarian. The vast majority of the three million refugees admitted to the country since 1945 have been from just three countries: Cuba, Vietnam, and the former Soviet Union.[2] For the United States, "refugee" has generally meant "refugee from Communism." From 1965 until 1980, this definition was actually written into the law.

During the 1930s, President Roosevelt clung resolutely to the established quota system as a reason for not opening the doors of the United States to those trying to flee Hitler's

Germany.[3] At the end of the war, the Allies struggled to figure out what to do with some one million displaced persons in the zones they occupied. The United States finally enacted the Displaced Persons Act (DPA), which allowed 205,000 refugees to be admitted between 1948 and 1950. The refugees would be charged against future years' quotas, instead of having to wait until quota spaces became available.

Provisions of the 1948 DPA also limited the ability of Jewish refugees to take advantage of it, although the 1950 renewal, which allowed another 200,000 displaced persons to enter, this time above the existing quota system, did enable some 80,000 Jewish refugees into the country. "Refugee" status was also granted to at least several thousand Nazi collaborators under the acts.[4] "Only a minority of those admitted . . . were Hitler's victims," concludes one analysis. "A larger number were members of groups that had supported the Third Reich or benefited from it . . . [In addition,] more than 70 percent . . . were refugees from the USSR and Eastern Europe."[5]

After the 1959 Cuban Revolution, the attorney general's office invoked its ability to "parole" thousands of Cubans who left the island. The 1966 Cuban Adjustment Act created a special legal situation just for Cubans: any Cuban who had been present for a year could be automatically granted legal permanent residence. Not only that, but a gamut of federal assistance programs facilitated Cubans' settlement in the United States.

For refugees from the neighboring island of Haiti, the U.S. extended a very different kind of welcome. Over the course of the 1970s thousands of Haitians fled the growing repression of the Duvalier dictatorship there and sought asylum in the United States. Many came on small rafts and homemade boats. By mid-1978 some six thousand to seven thousand cases had piled up before the INS (Immigration and Naturalization Service) office in Miami, as the office hesitated to act on them. After all, Duvalier was a U.S. ally—wouldn't it be contradictory to admit that his government was creating political refugees?

In July of that year, the INS intelligence division offered a blanket opinion that Haitians should be considered "economic," not political, refugees. To deter future migration, the INS enforcement office advised that Haitians be detained upon arrival, denied work permits, and be processed and expelled as quickly as possible. Under the new Haiti Program untrained officers began carrying out forty rapid-fire asylum interviews in a day. Over four thousand applications were processed under the program, and every one was denied.[6]

It was not until the Refugee Act of 1980 that the United States finally created a refugee policy that conformed to United Nations standards of treating equally all people facing political persecution. Even though the United States had signed the 1951 UN Convention and the 1967 Protocol defining refugees, its own policy remained a Cold War policy that applied only to refugees from Communist countries.

It didn't take long for the new Refugee Act to be tested. The stream of Haitian refugees continued, and only weeks after President Carter signed the law, thousands of Cuban refugees began arriving on the shores of South Florida. After a large group of Cubans occupied the Peruvian embassy in Havana demanding the right to emigrate to the United States, Fidel Castro reversed a long-standing policy of restricting emigration by sea and announced that those who wanted to leave were welcome to do so. Between April and September of 1980, some 125,000 Cubans departed, in what became known as the Mariel Boatlift, after the town from which many set sail.

Cuban immigrants arriving through the Mariel Boatlift were universally accepted as "political" refugees, while Haitians fleeing the violence of the Duvalier dictatorship at the same moment were denied refugee status, under the argument that they were leaving because of the economic devastation of the country. "Photographs of shirtless black refugees huddled aboard barely seaworthy craft evoked images buried deep in the American collective mind. Like the slave ships of yore, these boats also brought a cargo of black laborers, except that this time, they came on their own initiative, and this time, nobody wanted them. Still more pathetic were those black bodies washing ashore Florida's pristine beaches when their craft did not make it."[7]

In September 1981, President Reagan announced that Haitian immigrants posed a "serious national problem detrimental to the interests of the United States." He negotiated an agreement with the Duvalier dictatorship that allowed the Coast Guard to block immigration by patrolling Haitian waters and return all ships before they could reach U.S. territory.[8] No agreement like this existed anywhere else in the world.[9] By the end of 1990, 23,000 Haitians had been stopped at sea under the new policy, and only 8 of these were granted asylum.[10]

In one particularly glaring case, in July 1991 a large Haitian boat filled with refugees stopped to rescue some Cubans whose boat had wrecked at sea. When the Coast Guard intercepted them, the Haitian ship was returned with its passengers to Haiti—except for the Cubans, who were brought to Florida.[11]

At the heart of the policy divide between the warm welcome for Cubans and the cold one for Haitians was a logical leap that was rarely articulated. U.S. policy was based on the premise that in Communist countries, economic difficulties were the result of government policies, and were therefore political. Thus the Cubans who left in the early 1960s when faced with the threat of losing their property or their lifestyle, or those who left in the 1980s out of exhaustion from economic hardship, were political refugees: they were fleeing the policies of Cuba's Communist government.

In a capitalist country like Haiti, however, U.S. policy was based on the idea that poverty was merely an economic, not a political problem. Even Haitians who clearly faced direct political persecution—like Solivece Romet, who described his torture at the hands of the government-sponsored Tontons Macoutes and showed INS agents his scars—were classed as economic, rather than political refugees.[12] Those who made the mistake of telling INS agents that they intended to work if admitted to the United States were likewise doomed to the "economic" category and denied entry.

These events were eerily recapitulated in the summer of 1994, when a growing economic crisis in Cuba, including massive power outages, provoked another exodus from the island, coinciding with increasing desperation and repression by the military government that had overthrown President Jean-Bertrand Aristide in Haiti. The September 1991 coup in Haiti had provoked another huge wave of refugees in the last months of the year. Hundreds were dying in unseaworthy vessels. In November, amidst growing protests by Congress and human rights groups, a federal judge ordered the Bush administration to stop its long-standing policy of repatriating fleeing Haitians.[13]

Bush refused, however, to allow the refugees into the United States. Instead, ships intercepted at sea were taken to the U.S. naval base at Guantánamo Bay, Cuba. "Stories in the mainstream U.S. media continued to portray Guantánamo as a haven for refugees. Haitians, including the Haitian print and radio media, tended to refer to the base as a 'concentration camp,' a 'prison,' or, at best, 'a detention facility.' "[14]

The rationale for detaining and then repatriating the Haitians on Guantánamo rather than giving them the right to seek asylum in the United States was a curious one, but one that would become familiar later on. "While conceding that the Haitians are treated differently from other national groups who seek asylum in the United States, the Government claimed that the U.S. Constitution and other sources of U.S. and international law do not apply on Guantánamo."[15] The U.S. Refugee Act of 1980, and international law, were thus conveniently dispensed with, to the outrage of the UN High Commissioner for Refugees.[16]

In May 1992, with the camp overflowing, Bush reverted to the old Haiti Program: Haitians picked up at sea would once again be returned to Haiti. In the words of medical anthropologist, physician, and Partners in Health founder Paul Farmer, "Haiti resembled more and more a burning building with no exits."[17]

When President Bill Clinton took office in January 1993, he reversed Bush's policy of returning Haitians and reopened the Guantánamo camp. What he did not expect was a flood of Cuban rafters in the summer of 1994.

On August 18, 1994, with 21,000 Haitians in the makeshift camp, President Clinton did the unprecedented: he announced that Cubans picked up at sea, instead of being admitted to the United States, would join the Haitians at Guantánamo. "In a stroke, Clinton turned Cubans into the legal equivalent of Haitians," the *Washington Post* noted in wonderment.[18] By the end of 1994 some 50,000 refugees were housed there, at a cost of $500,000 to $1 million a day.[19]

Although the treatment was ostensibly equal, in fact it was not. In September 1994, U.S. troops occupied Haiti, and in November the massive repatriation of Haitians began, over the vociferous objections of immigrant and human rights organizations. Meanwhile in October, humanitarian evacuations began bringing Cubans from the camp into the United States. By the end of 1994, three-fourths of the Haitians had been "voluntarily" returned to Haiti, and in January 1995, those who refused were forcibly repatriated.[20]

In May 1995, the Clinton administration opened the way to admission for the 20,000 Cubans remaining in the camp. Only a few hundred Haitians were still in Guantánamo: most were unaccompanied children who had relatives or sponsors in the United States, pleading for them to be allowed in. Right as the doors were opened for Guantánamo's Cuban detainees, the repatriation of the Haitian children began. "Many of the children sent back to Haiti have been left to fend for themselves in squalid and dangerous conditions. Some are destitute and living in the street."[21]

The 1995 agreements that allowed the Cubans in did lead to the first small retreat from the welcome provided by the 1966 Cuban Adjustment Act. Clinton agreed to work with Castro to stem the tide. The new "wet foot, dry foot" policy announced in May 1995 allowed any Cuban who reached U.S. shores to continue to receive the preferential treatment of the 1966 act. Those picked up at sea, however, would be returned to Cuba. The United States also agreed to implement an orderly distribution of immigrant visas through its U.S. Interests Section in Havana (which is part of the Swiss embassy), to discourage people from seeking the dangerous sea route to immigration.

The case of refugees from Central America in the 1980s was similarly politicized.[22] After the 1979 Sandinista victory in Nicaragua, the right-wing governments of El Salvador and Guatemala stepped up their campaigns against leftist guerrillas and their supposed civilian supporters. In El Salvador, the FMLN rebels succeeded in gaining control of significant portions of the country's territory. Military raids against civilians in rebel-held territories, in addition to military and right-wing death squad repression against unarmed religious, social justice, and human rights activists, led to a mass exodus from the country.

In Guatemala, the smaller guerrilla groups operated mainly in isolated areas of the country, but the government and right-wing armed reaction was, if anything, more vicious. Hundreds of indigenous villages were destroyed in a scorched-earth policy that has been described as a genocide. Millions were internally displaced, and another million fled the country. Over the course of the 1980s, up to a million Salvadorans and Guatemalans sought refuge in the United States.

Because the United States opposed the revolutionary government in Nicaragua, and supported the right-wing governments in El Salvador and Guatemala, its response to refugees from the three countries could not have been more different. Between 1984 and 1990, 45,000 Salvadorans, 48,000 Nicaraguans, and 9,500 Guatemalans requested asylum; 26 percent of the Nicaraguan applications were approved, while only 2.6 percent of those submitted by Salvadorans and 1.8 percent of those submitted by Guatemalans were granted.[23] (Meanwhile, applicants from countries that the U.S. government considered enemies were approved at far higher rates: for Syrians, it was 73 percent; for people from the People's Republic of China, 52 percent.[24]) Thousands of refugees were arrested at the border and returned to Mexico without having the chance to even apply for asylum.

The Central American situation spawned a significant solidarity movement in the United States. Activists sought to end U.S. military support for the Contras in Nicaragua and for the governments of El Salvador and Guatemala. They worked with religious, human rights, and social justice organizations in Central America. Thousands of Americans traveled to Central America to learn firsthand about the situation, and to support the movements for social change there. They also created the Sanctuary Movement inside the United States, to provide refuge and aid for the thousands who came fleeing the violence there.

In 1985, a group of over eighty religious and refugee organizations brought suit against the federal government for unfairly applying its own laws regarding refugees in denying asylum applications by Guatemalan and Salvadoran refugees. Because of the leading role of the American Baptist Church, it became known as the ABC lawsuit. The decision in favor of the refugees, in December 1990, halted all deportations and granted Salvadorans and Guatemalans temporary legal status while they were allowed to resubmit their applications.[25]

Despite the ABC decision against the INS, and another 1990 ruling against the INS for "engag[ing] in a pattern and practice of pressuring or intimidating Salvadorans" to discourage them from applying for asylum, the 1996 immigration reforms imposed new obstacles for asylum applicants. For people already in the United States, a time limit was imposed: if they remained in the country for a year without filing an application, they lost their chance altogether. For those who arrived at the border and requested asylum, under the new rules they would either be denied summarily by whatever immigration agent they happened to encounter at the border, or they would be placed in detention while their case was investigated.[26]

Except Cubans. Even with the 1995 modifications, the Cuban Adjustment Act remained in place. To this day, Cubans are not detained, and they don't have to prove a well-founded fear of persecution. Like most pre-1924 immigrants, they just have to arrive here and say they want to come in.

PART THREE
IMMIGRATION AND RACE

Most people in the United States are unaware of the degree to which racial distinctions and exclusions have been embedded in U.S. history. Although the territory that is now the United States has been racially diverse ever since the first Europeans arrived, the political entity of the *country* was restricted to people from Europe. Even today, sources from textbooks to popular culture promote the idea that the real essence of the country is white. The oft-repeated phrase "this is a country of immigrants" reaffirms that notion. The "immigrants" it refers to are European immigrants. Only by a large stretch of the imagination could Native Americans, or enslaved Africans, be included in the category "immigrants." U.S. immigration and naturalization policy was one piece of a national political structure and identity aimed deliberately at creating, and preserving, a white country. The legacies of this history are very much with us still today.

MYTH 10

THE UNITED STATES IS A MELTING POT THAT HAS ALWAYS WELCOMED IMMIGRANTS FROM ALL OVER THE WORLD

In most of the world, the concepts of race and nation are very closely connected. In the nineteenth century, when the first nation-states of Europe were coming into existence, the two terms were often used interchangeably: "the French race" or "the German race." Borders, and governments, were supposed to reflect "nations" that were unified by historical, linguistic, and cultural ties that were often thought of in terms of bloodlines.

Even in Europe, these ideas were very problematic. Since Europe was populated by waves of migration and conquest from the Mediterranean and from Central Asia over the course of many centuries, nowhere did a really homogenous population exist. Spain emerged as an apparently coherent entity in the 1400s only by driving out Muslims and Jews, and by declaring one of the many dialects of the peninsula to be the official language. Ethnic nationalist movements even today, like those in the Basque Country and Catalonia in Spain's northwest and northeast, respectively, still challenge the hegemony of Spanish language and government. Most European conflicts of the twentieth century were the result of groups trying to enforce some kind of racial, ethnic, or cultural purity, or to define exactly where the borders of one nation end and those of another begin.

Most histories of the United States portray its national identity very differently, as a melting pot made up of ethnically diverse immigrants. The citizenship test reveals what most people believe to be the basis of U.S. nationality. To become a citizen, you have to demonstrate knowledge of English and knowledge of certain aspects of U.S. history and institutions. There are no racial or ethnic requirements.

But in fact U.S. nationality has historically been based very much on race. Congress first enacted a naturalization law—determining who could become a citizen of the United States—in 1790, fourteen years after the country was established. The law restricted naturalization to "free white persons." "White" was not defined—its meaning was thought to be obvious. Neither, for that matter, was "persons"—but it went without saying that "persons" meant "male persons." With the growth of racial pseudoscience in the nineteenth century, Congress and the courts were increasingly drawn into trying to define who was and was not racially "white" and therefore eligible for citizenship.

There were many people, though, who were definitively not white, yet were present in the newly established country. Native Americans, even if physically present in the new country, were considered permanent foreigners belonging to different nations. The United States was established as a country based on slavery, and in order to justify slavery, those enslaved had to be denied the rights of citizenship.

But slavery and race were also intertwined. If slaves had no legal rights, what about blacks who were not legally enslaved? Some states abolished slavery shortly after independence, and some granted citizenship to free blacks, but that did not make them citizens of the United States. People of African origin, whether slave or free, were nonpersons as far as the federal government was concerned. The relationship of nationality and race was very firmly established. The "nation" remained clearly defined as an entity composed of white people.

Events in the 1800s entrenched the restriction of rights to white people. The Fugitive Slave Act, state immigration laws, and the Dred Scott decision raise interesting parallels to today's debate on immigration. The Fugitive Slave Act, passed by Congress in 1850, required residents of non-slave states to enforce the institution by assisting in the arrest and return of former slaves who sought freedom in states where slavery was illegal. The federal government thus prohibited equal rights, and equal treatment, in all states. Even if a state wanted to grant equal rights, it could not. The law essentially criminalized those who treated blacks as human beings rather than as property—just as some immigration proposals today propose to criminalize those who treat immigrants as human beings.[1]

Although some of the older non-slave states argued for

the rights of all persons, the laws of many non-slave states actually prohibited African Americans from moving there at all, though these laws were not always enforced. Illinois, Ohio, Michigan, Indiana, California, and Oregon all passed legislation as they became states that banned African American immigration. The Illinois state constitution passed in 1848 required the legislature to "prohibit free persons of color from immigrating to and settling in this state."[2] Indiana voters—and only whites could vote, of course—approved a law written during the state's Constitutional Convention in 1850–51 that prohibited African Americans from entering the state. And Article 13 of the state's constitution made it illegal for employers to hire African Americans.[3]

As early as the 1790s, when there were only about sixty thousand free blacks in U.S. territory, state and federal governments had begun looking for ways to eliminate this unwanted population. In 1819 the federal government amended the law prohibiting the slave trade to ensure that captured enslaved Africans would not be admitted to the United States. Colonization schemes at the state and national levels attempting to deport free blacks littered the nineteenth century. Luminaries from Francis Scott Key to Daniel Webster to Andrew Jackson sponsored the American Society for Colonizing the Free People of Color in the United States (ACS), and southern states pursued the project of deporting manumitted (freed) slaves, as did Abraham Lincoln. Over its fifty years of existence, the ACS "resettled over 1,000 captives from slave ships and sponsored the transportation of 12,000 Negroes, most of them recently manumitted from the large estates in the Deep South, under conditions close to deportation."[4]

In 1857, the Supreme Court ruled that a person descended from Africans could not be a citizen of the United States, and thus could not have rights under U.S. laws. Dred Scott was born a slave in Virginia, but lived as a free man when he moved with his master to Illinois and the Wisconsin territories, where slavery was prohibited. When the master's family tried to reenslave him in Missouri, he sued for his freedom. The court decision was very clear: even after being emancipated, the descendants of Africans could not be citizens.

In the court's opinion, Justice Taney wrote that the framers of the Constitution clearly intended to refer to *white* people when they guaranteed rights and privileges to all citizens. Blacks, Taney explained,

> had for more than a century before been regarded as beings of an inferior order, and altogether unfit to associate with the white race either in social or political relations, and so far inferior that they had no rights which the white man was bound to respect . . . This opinion was at that time fixed and universal in the civilized portion of the white race. It was regarded as an axiom in morals as well as in politics which no one thought of disputing or supposed to be open to dispute, and men in every grade and position in society daily

> and habitually acted upon it in their private pursuits, as well as in matters of public concern, without doubting for a moment the correctness of this opinion.[5]

Thus spoke the judge. The job of the Court was to uphold the intent of the Constitution—which was to deny rights and citizenship to people of African descent. As for the Declaration of Independence, the justice further explained, "it is too clear for dispute that the enslaved African race were not intended to be included, and formed no part of the people who framed and adopted this declaration."[6]

Whites were part of the community of "men" by virtue of being here. Blacks were excluded from the community of "men" by virtue of having been enslaved by white people. Arguments about the rights of citizens and "aliens" today reflect many of the same ideas. Immigrants may be physically present—as African Americans were—but they are excluded from the community that is accorded rights. Rights are reserved for the portion of the population defined as "citizens."

Post–Civil War legislation took a first step away from white exclusivity by implementing the notion of citizenship by virtue of birth in the United States, and by nominally extending naturalization privileges to people of African origin. The Civil Rights Act of 1866 redefined citizenship by stating that "All persons born . . . in the United States and not subject to any foreign power, excluding Indians not taxed, are declared to be citizens of the United States." The Fourteenth Amendment further clarified this in 1868, stating that "All persons born or naturalized in the US, and subject to the jurisdiction thereof, are citizens of the US and of the state wherein they reside." The exclusion of Native Americans reiterated by the "and subject to the jurisdiction thereof" clause was upheld by the Supreme Court in 1884. It was not until 1940 that the last restrictions on Native American citizenship and naturalization were removed.[7]

Except in the case of Native Americans, these acts seemed to privilege the place of birth of the individual, rather than "race" or the place of birth of parents or ancestors, as the key to citizenship. (Children of U.S. citizens, however, were automatically granted citizenship even if born outside of the country.) But they still made it clear that rights apply only to some people, not to all people.

Racial/national exclusion still applied to naturalization: only *some* people were eligible to be naturalized. U.S. law restricted naturalization to people who were "white" until 1870, when it added the category of people of "African nativity or African descent." Because there was virtually no immigration from Africa until much later in the twentieth century, this addition was essentially meaningless—in practice, naturalization was still limited to white Europeans.

The framers of the Constitution may have had Englishmen in mind when they wrote "all men." The authors of the Fourteenth Amendment clearly had two categories in mind when they wrote "all persons": whites, and the descendants of African slaves. But they wrote the Amendment just as a new wave of immigrants was about to enter the country. How would U.S. law and society respond to newcomers who arrived from Canada, from Europe, but also from Asia and from Latin America (primarily Mexico) after 1868? If people who were not white were not allowed to become citizens, were they still allowed to come to the United States?

In 1882, Congress answered with a resounding "no" by passing the Chinese Exclusion Act. As "aliens ineligible to citizenship," the Chinese, and other groups that followed, such as Japanese people and other Asians, were stripped of other rights as well. The Fourteenth Amendment prohibited discrimination based on race, but it did not prohibit discrimination based on citizenship status—and access to citizenship was still very clearly based on race. The Chinese-origin population fell from a high of 118,746 in 1900 to 85,202 in 1930. Political scientist Aristide Zolberg described this "willful reduction of a national group" as "the only successful instance of 'ethnic cleansing' in the history of American immigration."[8]

California and ten other states banned Japanese residents from owning land through a prohibition on land ownership by "aliens ineligible to citizenship." Arkansas was even more specific, declaring that "no Japanese or a descendant of a Japanese shall ever purchase or hold title to any lands in the State of Arkansas." A 1907 federal law stipulated that a female citizen who married an alien would be stripped of her own status as a citizen, and a 1922 revision that allowed such women to retain their citizenship still removed it from women who married aliens who were racially ineligible for citizenship. (Not until 1940 was a woman's citizenship status made completely independent of her husband's.)[9]

In 1923, the Supreme Court ruled that Asian Indians were not eligible for citizenship. The federal government immediately "began a campaign to strip naturalized Asian Indians of their citizenship." California expanded its ban on land ownership to Asian Indians. Suddenly, a group of people with rights became a group of people without rights—because the court had ruled that they were not white.[10]

The immigration restriction laws of 1917, 1921, and 1924 codified these racial/national exclusions. Most accounts describe these laws as aimed against southern and eastern Europeans, who made up the majority of people migrating to the country at the time. What is less remembered in the history books is how these laws treated non-Europeans. The 1917 Immigration Act, most commonly known because it instated a literacy requirement, also created a "barred Asiatic zone" that covered most of the world's territory, from Afghanistan to the Pacific. Chinese and Japanese immigrants had already been completely excluded and declared ineligible for citizenship; now all people defined as Asian were excluded.

The 1921 and 1924 acts created numerical limits based on "national origins"—but only of white people. The 1924 act looked at the "national origins" of the population of the country as revealing the correct balance between northwestern and southeastern Europeans. Allowing for a total of 155,000 immigrants a year, it divided them proportionally by country—16 percent to come from southern and eastern Europe, and 84 percent from northern and western Europe.[11]

In designing these acts, Congress made it clear that, despite the Fourteenth Amendment and the extension of citizenship and even naturalization to people of African origin, this was essentially a white country. The presence of people who were not white was incidental, not central, to its composition. So when the population was examined in order to determine its "national origins," it was only the white population that was counted. People who were "the descendants of slave immigrants," and "aliens ineligible for citizenship or their descendants" (i.e., people from the "barred Asiatic zone") were simply not counted—and they got no quotas.[12]

(Something similar happens today in the U.S. census. When it counts people of Hispanic origin in the United States, it excludes Puerto Ricans living in Puerto Rico. They're citizens—but somehow they're different from other citizens, and thus not counted.[13])

The quotas did limit the immigration of southeastern Europeans and privilege those from northern Europe. But it's a sign of just how much our history books accept the idea that the United States is a white country that the law's prohibitions against people who were not white is usually not even mentioned. The quota system established by the 1924 law remained in effect until 1965.

The law listed sixty-four countries of the world outside of the Western Hemisphere, with their corresponding quotas. The minimum quota was 100, and thirty-nine countries

—primarily those in Asia and Africa—received the minimum. Great Britain and Northern Ireland, and Germany, topped the list with 65,721 and 25,957, respectively, followed by the Irish Free State with 17,853. The other countries of Europe received between 1,000 and 6,500 slots.[14]

(Just to add to the confusion, Asian countries like China and India got the minimum hundred-person quota—but Chinese and Indians were still prohibited from immigrating. So the quota was more symbolic than real.)

It was not until the 1940s that people other than whites and those of African descent were, gradually, afforded the right to naturalize (though not necessarily to immigrate): first Native Americans (in 1940), then Chinese (1943), then Filipinos and Indians (1946). Finally, in 1952, all racial/national restrictions to citizenship were lifted. Part of the probable impetus for expanding the categories of those eligible for citizenship was embarrassment at being the only country in the world besides Hitler's Germany to uphold such a racially exclusive definition of citizenship.[15]

What, then, was the status of those in the United States who did not belong to one of the two categories—whites and people of African descent—allowed to be citizens between 1870 and 1940? It's worth noting that the two categories themselves are somewhat unwieldy. One refers to a race—without specifying how that race is defined—and the other refers to a birthplace.

In the wake of the post–Civil War upsurge in immigration, it fell to U.S. courts to decide who, in fact, belonged to the "white race." Would it be decided by skin tone? National origin? A combination of the two? In either case, exactly where and how would the lines be drawn? Was the Japanese man who showed the court the "pinkish" hue to his skin white? What about the Syrian, who complained that since he hailed from the land of Jesus Christ, denying his whiteness would be like denying that Jesus was white? Or Armenians, whom the law classed as nonwhite until 1909, and white subsequently? Between 1878 and 1952—when the racial requirement for citizenship was overturned—dozens of individuals sought to establish their race, and the courts became more and more involved in making decisions in individual cases that then became the basis for policy.

The immigration and naturalization restrictions constituted a neat circumvention of the Fourteenth Amendment. The amendment guaranteed equal rights to all citizens—but it did not specify that all people should have equal access to citizenship. In the Dred Scott decision, the court ruled that it was obvious that "all men" did not include blacks. Now, states could not "make or enforce any law which shall abridge the privileges or immunities of citizens of the United States." But if only whites and people of African ancestry could be citizens, the amendment still allowed groups of people to be excluded from rights based on race.

Mae Ngai argues that "unlike Euro-Americans, whose ethnic and racial identities became uncoupled during the 1920s, Asians' and Mexicans' ethnic and racial identities remained conjoined. The legal racialization of these ethnic groups' national origin cast them as permanently foreign and unassimilable to the nation . . . These racial formations produced 'alien citizens'—Asian Americans and Mexican Americans born in the United States with formal U.S. citizenship but who remained alien in the eyes of the nation."[16]

The experience of African Americans further illustrates this notion of "alien citizens." Legally granted the rights of citizenship during Reconstruction, they were also subject to a new wave of exclusionism during the period between 1890 to the 1930s, which historians refer to as the "nadir of race relations" in the postemancipation period.[17] The wave of immigration from southern and eastern Europe and U.S. expansion, which incorporated new nonwhite peoples under U.S. rule, contributed to a hardening of the racial boundaries of citizenship. Whites, who were voluntary immigrants, were people inherently eligible for citizenship. Nonwhites, who were to be conquered and exploited, were not.

Civil rights legislation passed in the 1950s and 1960s furthered the job begun in the 1860s of creating a legal basis for racial equality. The immigration reforms of the 1960s (discussed in Part One) ostensibly created racial equality in immigration policy as well, by granting equal quotas to all countries.

Nevertheless, the historical structures that privileged white people continued to shape social realities and even immigration policy. Congress enshrined its continuing belief that the country needed more white people in the new "diversity visa" program established in 1992, in the context of the large Asian and Latin American immigration since 1965. The program set aside fifty-five thousand visas to be granted to citizens of countries that were underrepresented in the number of immigrants they sent.

In arguing for the legislation, Senator Alfonse D'Amato pointed to the "painful, and even tragic problems for Irish, Germans, Italians, Poles, and others without immediate family members in the United States." During the first two years of the program, 40 percent of the visas were reserved for Irish immigrants.[18] In 1995 the program was expanded to include all "underrepresented" countries—or rather, to exclude "overrepresented" countries. Countries that had sent over 50,000 immigrants to the United States in the previous five years were specifically excluded. As of 2006, those countries excluded were Canada, mainland China, Colombia, the Dominican Republic, El Salvador, Haiti, India, Jamaica, Mexico, Pakistan, the Philippines, Poland, Russia, South Korea, the United Kingdom and its dependent territories *except Northern Ireland*, and Vietnam.[19]

While the diversity program is a small piece of U.S. immigration policy, it nevertheless responds to a deep and long-standing assumption in U.S. history: that whites are the true citizens here. If non-Europeans have not assimilated in the same way that Europeans have, it's because everything from the Constitution to immigration and naturalization law, to the political, social, and economic factors discussed in the next two chapters has been founded on and perpetrated the notion that the United States is, and should be, a white country.

MYTH 11

SINCE WE ARE ALL THE DESCENDANTS OF IMMIGRANTS HERE, WE ALL START ON EQUAL FOOTING

The United States has incorporated populations through voluntary immigration, involuntary immigration, and conquest. Saying it is a nation of immigrants obscures the latter two types of population incorporation. Even voluntary immigration includes some people who lack rights: contract workers, indentured servants, braceros. When people compare today's immigrants to previous generations, they are generally using the model of white European voluntary immigrants as the comparison. The law privileged white European immigrants from the beginning.

Immigrants of color share many characteristics with those forcibly incorporated into the country, including Native Americans, African Americans, Mexicans, and Puerto Ricans. Scholars of ethnic studies have used the terms "internal colonialism" or "colonized minorities" to explain the way people of color have been incorporated into the United States. Latin American and Asian immigrants are entering a society that has historically defined itself against their ancestors, and through the conquest of their ancestors. Customs, beliefs, and laws that constructed people of color as subject peoples rather than potential citizens, to be admitted or excluded according to the needs of U.S. employers, have extended into the twenty-first century.

The United States came into existence through a process of English conquest of lands inhabited by Native Americans. From the first English settlement until 1898, the ideology of conquest, and of the fitness of English and English-descended people to rule over others, was virtually unquestioned among the country's leaders. Commentators in the 1890s spoke unashamedly of the unique capacity of the "Anglo-Saxon race" for self-government, and its need for expansion. "The Anglo-Saxon race," a columnist for the *Atlantic Monthly* wrote in 1898, "now holds the foremost place in the world . . . It stands for the best yet reached in ideas and institutions, the highest type of civilization . . . Our own best interests imperatively demand that we should maintain the Anglo-Saxon race in the occupation of every foot of land which it now justly holds anywhere on the globe, and that wherever we can do so righteously, we should endeavor to increase its influence and its possessions."[1]

Historian and philosopher John Fiske spoke for many when he emphasized the English nature of the United States. "The indomitable spirit of English liberty is alike indomitable in every land where men of English race have set their feet as masters," he wrote. "The conquest of the North American continent by men of English race was unquestionably the most prodigious event in the political annals of man kind." The American Revolution "was not a struggle by two different peoples," rather "it was sustained by a part of the English people in behalf of principles that time has shown to be equally dear to all." The American Revolution, in fact, "made it apparent to an astonished world that instead of *one* there were now *two Englands*, alike prepared to work with might and main toward the political regeneration of mankind [emphasis in original]."[2]

Furthermore, the Anglo-Saxon race was destined to migrate—in fact, because it was the superior race, its migration would be the salvation of every part of the world it moved to. It was not migrating to assimilate, it was migrating to dominate. In the words of Josiah Strong, secretary of the Congregational Home Missionary Society, in his influential 1885 book *Our Country*, the Anglo-Saxon had "an instinct or genius for colonizing. His unequaled energy, his indomitable perseverance, and his personal independence, made him a pioneer. He excels all others in pushing his way into new countries." As "the highest civilization—having developed peculiarly aggressive traits calculated to impress its institutions upon mankind," the Anglo-Saxon race "will spread itself over the earth.

"This powerful race will move down upon Mexico, down upon Central and South America, out upon the islands of the sea, over upon Africa and beyond. And can any one doubt that the results of this competition of races will be the 'survival of the fittest?' "[3] Anglo-Saxons, then, were supposed to migrate, and to conquer everyone in their path. Non-Anglo-Saxons were supposed to stay put and be conquered—

unless Anglo-Saxons decided to move them around to serve as a labor force.

Anglo-Saxonism justified U.S. imperial expansion; it also nurtured racism against the southern and eastern European immigrants who were entering the United States at the same time. These racisms were intertwined, though not identical. European immigrants were "in-between," identified in "semi-racial" ways. Italians were called "guineas"—in a derogatory reference to their supposed closeness to Africa; "Huns" and Slavic peoples were suspiciously Asiatic. Between the 1910s and the 1930s, however, all of these people "became white"—as part of the same process that reiterated the exclusion of those who could never be white.[4]

When the national origins quotas for immigration were implemented in the 1920s, the Western Hemisphere was conspicuously left out of the calculations. Not because Mexicans were considered potential members of U.S. society—quite the contrary. Mexicans were omitted from the exclusionary legislation because industry and agriculture in the Southwest depended on their labor, just as it depended on their less-than-full-citizen status.

Mexican Americans were first incorporated into the country with the annexation of Texas in 1845, and then under the Treaty of Guadalupe Hidalgo that ended the Mexican-American War in 1848 and granted the United States 55 percent of Mexico's territory. Prior to the reforms of the 1860s, citizenship was still reserved for whites. Yet Guadalupe Hidalgo offered citizenship to Mexicans living in the newly acquired territories. What was the logic for granting citizenship to these newly conquered peoples?

For one thing, annexation carefully encompassed the least populated areas of Mexico and stopped where the population started to increase.[5] There were some 80,000 to 100,000 Mexican nationals in the territory taken in 1848, in addition to uncounted numbers of Native Americans.[6] In the racial worldview of the Anglo-Saxon conquerors, Mexicans were an anomaly: not white, not black, not Indian, not Asian. By being granted citizenship, Mexicans were tacitly accepted as white, even though they had just been conquered under the rationale of Anglo-Saxon expansion and Manifest Destiny. "The whole race of Mexicans here is becoming a useless commodity," wrote the *Galveston Weekly News* in 1855. Lynchings, vigilante justice, and land dispossession confirmed the racialized way in which Anglos viewed Mexicans.[7]

Official confusion about Mexicans' racial character was compounded in the 1920s, when people of Mexican descent who came to the United States as immigrants were even allowed to naturalize (unlike Asians). In 1929 the secretary of labor explained, "The Mexican people are of such a mixed stock and individuals have such a limited knowledge of their racial composition that it would be impossible for the most learned and experienced ethnologist or anthropologist to classify or determine their racial origin. Thus, making an effort to exclude them from admission or citizenship because of their racial status is practically impossible."[8]

Mexican Americans learned, as African Americans did several decades later, that even citizenship was no guarantee of equal rights. Socially and legally, these new citizens who were not Anglo-American occupied a distinctly second-class status. Like African Americans, Mexican Americans were barred from jobs, from schools, from public facilities, from land ownership, from residential areas. As David Gutiérrez writes, "within two decades of the American conquest it had become clear that, with few exceptions, Mexican Americans had been relegated to a stigmatized, subordinate position in the social and economic hierarchies."[9]

Strange as it seems, prior to the 1920s the new border between Mexico and the United States was open and unmonitored. "Immigration" and the laws governing immigration referred to those who arrived by sea in New York or California. White U.S. citizens had been migrating—undocumented—to Texas and other parts of Mexico since the early 1800s. In fact it was Anglo immigrants in Texas who rebelled against the Mexican government to declare the independent Texas Republic, and U.S. citizens who crossed into Mexico without permission who fought the Mexican-American war.

The Anglo-Americans who immigrated to Mexico clearly saw themselves as colonizers, and their goal as conquering, not assimilating into, their new homeland. "Texas should be effectually and fully Americanized," wrote Stephen Austin in 1835, "in language, political principles, common origin, sympathy, and even interest."[10]

The development of mining, agriculture, and railroads

in the Mexican north and the U.S. west was a linked venture: U.S. capital operated on both sides of the border, and Mexicans moved back and forth rather fluidly. A transborder railroad completed in 1890 further facilitated movement.[11] "Immigration inspectors ignored Mexicans coming into the southwestern United States during the 1900s and 1910s" because the U.S. government "did not seriously consider Mexican immigration within its purview." Only beginning in 1919 did Mexicans have to formally pass through an immigration station and request permission to enter.[12]

Labor recruitment in Mexico was not inhibited by the 1885 Contract Labor Law prohibiting foreign recruitment, which, like other restrictive measures, was aimed primarily at Europe and China. In fact, the Chinese Exclusion Act and the prohibition on contract labor led employers to actively recruit Mexican workers deep in the interior of Mexico for the first time. Now Mexican workers in the United States did not come just from the already fluid, integrated border region. A true migrant stream from the interior of Mexico into the interior of the United States, including areas of the Midwest like Kansas and Chicago, was established.[13]

The 1917 Immigration Act, which imposed a literacy requirement and a head tax on immigrants, also created explicit provisions for Mexicans to be exempted from these so that southwestern agricultural interests could continue to import them as temporary workers. It was the first "guest worker" program, and it illustrates the tangled network of immigration legality. It remained in place until 1922.[14] Puerto Rican labor migration was also strengthened in 1917, with the unilateral granting of U.S. citizenship to inhabitants of the island.

Although the 1924 national quota law did not place a numerical restriction on Mexican immigration, it made a fundamental change in the way immigration was to be dealt with. Instead of a basically open border and welcoming attitude toward immigrants—including Mexicans, who were considered nominally "white" and therefore eligible for citizenship—the 1924 law closed the border and demanded that every potential immigrant be scrutinized. It created two new things that now seem to be a natural part of our immigration policy: the Border Patrol and deportation. In the process, it also created the category of the "illegal immigrant."

Prior to 1924, immigrants could be deported for committing certain crimes, but with an open border there was no such thing as illegal entry or an "illegal" immigrant. The 1924 law made "unlawful entry" a crime and created a new police force, the Border Patrol, to prevent and punish it. Suddenly, there was a new legal category of people in the country: not citizens, not immigrants. They were people entirely without rights. And almost all of them were Mexican—those people without a race who couldn't be denied citizenship or excluded on a racial basis. Now there was a new rationale for excluding them.

Racial exclusions from citizenship were removed in 1952, and Congress revised the national origins quotas in 1965. Legalized segregation and second-class citizenship based on race were also dismantled at the federal level in the 1950s and '60s. But the Border Patrol, the policy of deportation, and the concept of the "illegal immigrant" were here to stay.

Mexicans became the ultimate subject labor force, especially for seasonal agricultural work. Employers, and the government, could perfectly control the labor supply, first opening the gates and then closing them, deporting workers when the season ended or when the depression began. Over 400,000 people of Mexican origin were deported during the early 1930s, some 60 percent of them U.S. citizens.[15]

The 1942 bracero program reaffirmed the role of Mexicans as workers to be imported and exported according to the needs of U.S. agribusiness rather than as humans with rights. A similar program, the British West Indian Program, brought temporary workers from the Caribbean to work in agriculture on the East Coast from 1943 to 1952. The 1952 immigration overhaul created yet another method for bringing in temporary workers: the H-2 program, which allowed for the contracting of temporary agricultural workers. The H-2 program was later divided into H-2A for agricultural workers and H-2B for other temporary, seasonal workers and continues in existence to this day. Because West Coast growers already had other systems in place, the H-2 program was used primarily by East Coast agriculture. In 1999, almost half of the nearly 30,000 H-2B visa entries worked in the Southeast, mostly in tobacco. The top states using the program were North Carolina (by far the largest, with over 10,000 H-2 workers), Georgia, and Virginia.[16]

Initially, the H-2 program brought workers primarily from the Caribbean. Interestingly, it was implemented just as British West Indians were excluded from actually immigrating under the Immigration and Nationality Act of 1952. The INA specifically stipulated that residents of Britain's colonies would not be considered eligible as immigrants under the quota assigned to Great Britain—even though they were British. It was an eerie recapitulation of the rationale of slavery: we want black people to come here to work, but we won't consider them potential citizens.

"Operation Wetback" in 1954, in which over a million Mexicans were deported, provides another example of the dueling logic of U.S. attitudes toward Mexicans. It occurred in the midst of the bracero program, which was bringing about 200,000 Mexicans a year into the country as guest workers. The deportations meant that there were fewer workers available for agriculture, and that more were recruited as braceros—about 300,000 in 1954, and 400,000 to 450,000 a year in subsequent years.[17] Deportations and recruitment served the same purpose: they provided workers, but ensured that the workers remained "aliens" without rights. And they reinforced the notion that citizens and people with rights were white people.

Operation Wetback occurred in the same year that *Brown v. Board of Education* marked the resurgence of a movement for rights for black people—a concept that had been experimented with during Reconstruction and then submerged for several generations. As in the past, the tentative expansion of rights for some was accompanied by simultaneous repression, making it clear that the concept of rights was still an exclusionary one.

When the bracero program (which served mostly the Southwest) was ended in 1964, the demand for cheap, exploitable, temporary workers didn't evaporate—in fact it was increasing, due to the structural changes in the economy described earlier. Over its twenty-two-year life, the program had brought some five million Mexican workers into the country.[18] So a new category for filling that demand emerged: workers who were deemed "illegal."

They may have been crossing the border legally to do agricultural work for decades. Their employers were still recruiting them, and they still needed the work. But with the stroke of a pen, they lost even the meager rights offered under the bracero program. Suddenly, they were "illegal." It seemed the United States couldn't live with imported Mexican workers, and couldn't live without them.

The civil rights impulse that was restoring or extending some rights to black citizens, and creating national unease with the guest-worker program, ended at the bounds of "legality." Agribusiness could live with civil rights, as long as it could also be assured of a workforce without rights. The AFL-CIO and even, for a time, the United Farm Workers union, went along with the notion. As long as popular opinion accepted the division between "legal" and "illegal," the social structures of inequality—and the profits they facilitated—could continue.

Starting in the 1990s, the numbers of workers brought in on the H-2 program rose sharply, and recruitment shifted from the Caribbean to Mexico. By 1999, 96 percent of H-2 workers came from Mexico.[19] In the well-established pattern, recruitment programs set off a stream of migrants: precisely those states that were bringing in large numbers of temporary workers from Mexico in the 1990s began to see increases in permanent migration in the 2000s. By 2004 these three recent destinations for immigrants were each estimated to have from 200,000 to 300,000 undocumented immigrants.[20] Between 1980 and 1990, the foreign-born population rose from 1.3 percent to 1.7 percent in North Carolina, 1.7 percent to 2.7 percent in Georgia, and 3.3 percent to 5 percent in Virginia.[21] By 2003, the foreign born had reached 6.2 percent in North Carolina, 7.9 percent in Georgia, and 9.2 percent in Virginia.[22] By 2005, the proportions were 7.0 percent in North Carolina, 8.8 percent in Georgia, and 9.7 percent in Virginia—and they ranked fourteenth, ninth, and eleventh, respectively, in numbers of immigrants by state.[23]

Today's immigrants, then, are heirs to a long history of immigration and expansion that has incorporated people into the country's population in a distinctly unequal manner. Today's immigrants are still immigrants, like the Europeans of a century ago. But they are also Asians and Latinos, whose history in the United States has been one of exclusion and conquest. Both of these intertwined histories structure the ways in which today's immigrants come to, and are received by, U.S. society today.

MYTH 12

TODAY'S IMMIGRANTS THREATEN THE NATIONAL CULTURE BECAUSE THEY ARE NOT ASSIMILATING

In 1993, Toni Morrison wrote, in a special issue of *Time* magazine on immigration, that the "most enduring and efficient rite of passage into American culture" for immigrants was "negative appraisals of the native-born black population. Only when the lesson of racial estrangement is learned is assimilation complete." Blacks, she said, were permanent noncitizens. "The move into mainstream America always means buying into the notion of American blacks as the real aliens."[1]

Italian, Polish, and Jewish immigrants may not have identified with, or been accepted into, white society when they first arrived in the United States. But they, or more often their children, assimilated by becoming "white" and experienced upward mobility as they melded into the white majority. And part of the assimilation into whiteness meant the adoption of white racial attitudes.

Black Puerto Rican author Piri Thomas described the generational gap among Italians in his Bronx neighborhood in the 1940s: the mothers and grandmothers accepted him as one of their own while the new generation attacked him as a "spic." One of the Italian boys speculated that if Piri had a sister, they could "cover the bitch's face with the flag an' fuck 'er for old glory," in a graphic rendering of Toni Morrison's point.[2]

James Loewen points out that just as European immigrants moved out of their inner-city enclaves and merged into white America, African Americans were being residentially segregated as the phenomenon of "sundown towns," which explicitly prohibited blacks from remaining in them after the sun set, spread across the country.[3] Assimilation for people of European origin was accompanied by ongoing exclusion of people of color already in the United States.

For immigrants of color, assimilation means something very different than it historically has for European immigrants. For Latin American immigrants, assimilation more often means shedding their American dream and joining the lowest rungs in a caste-like society where Native Americans and African Americans, the most "assimilated" people of color, have been consistently kept at the bottom. When Haitian immigrants assimilate, explains one study, "they become not generic, mainstream Americans but specifically African Americans and primarily the poor African Americans most vulnerable to American racism."[4]

As Toni Morrison suggested, racial inequality is so deeply embedded in the national culture and social fabric of the United States that assimilation has historically meant finding, learning, and accepting one's place in the racial order. If new immigrants could succeed in challenging and transforming the racial order of the United States, that would be a good thing. But the signs do not point in that direction. The current anti-immigrant sentiment reinforces racial inequality.

The United States, as we have seen, defined itself from the first as a white, Anglo-Saxon country. Africans and Native Americans may have lived in the territories claimed by the United States, but they were not citizens. The Mexicans—primarily people of Spanish and Native American origin—who were added to the U.S. population with the 1848 conquest were granted citizenship, of a sort—but without shaking the firmly held idea that the United States was an Anglo-Saxon country.

The new, non-Anglo-Saxon immigrants, starting with the Irish in the 1850s and growing with the southern and eastern Europeans from the 1870s on, were neither Anglo-Saxons nor people of color. Many of these new European immigrants came from nations that Anglo-Saxons considered inferior, and many of them came from peoples without states. They were oppressed minorities in the countries or empires they came from. Many came from the Ottoman Empire or the Austro-Hungarian Empire. Many were Irish, from a land controlled by England, or they were Jews from Eastern Europe. Some were southern Italians, in a country only just unified, where the South was economically dependent on the North.

When European immigrants assimilated, they joined white society in social and cultural terms. Obviously, the color of their skin did not change—but the category of "white" expanded from its former association with Anglo-Saxons to include these newcomers. Anglo-Saxonism was fundamentally based on the domination of Africans, Native Americans, and Asians, and the institutions and ideologies of the United States reflected this reality. Southern and eastern Europeans were not originally part of this racial dynamic. Assimilating into it meant accepting it and identifying with the racial inequality it entailed—insisting, successfully, on their place among whites.

When Asian and Latino immigrants assimilate, they also assimilate to the United States racial hierarchy, but in a different way. Very few of them can cross the line into whiteness. Instead, they assimilate by becoming people of color in a racially divided society. Assimilation, instead of bringing upward mobility, brings downward mobility. Of course there are exceptions, but overwhelmingly, the social and economic statistics have told the same dreary story for many generations: blacks, Hispanics, and Native Americans are at the bottom of the social hierarchy, even—perhaps especially—those whose ancestors have the longest presence in the country. It's not lack of assimilation that keeps them marginalized—it's assimilation itself.

The relationship between assimilation and downward mobility has been especially noted in studies of schoolchildren. Education professor Marcelo Suárez-Orozco conducted two major studies of Latino adolescents in which he found that the most recent immigrants tended to be the students with the highest aspirations and the strongest belief in the American dream. This was because, as immigrants, they were not yet educated into the U.S. racial order. Teachers consistently reported on new immigrants' commitment to education, their work ethic, and their respect for their teachers. As they became more Americanized, they entered an oppositional inner-city teenage culture that valued money, drugs, and reckless behaviors defined as cool—the opposite of the hopeful and hard-working recent arrivals.

Over time new immigrants lost their optimism. They became acculturated by becoming aware of the long-standing historical place of Latinos in U.S. society. They realized that education was not the solution they had originally believed it was. In fact, studies have shown that the higher the educational level, the greater the income disparity between whites and nonwhites in U.S. society. Rather than leveling the playing field, educational achievement maintains or even exacerbates inequalities.[5]

Although students of color may not be aware of the statistics, their decisions seem to reflect a larger awareness that education is not an automatic ticket to the American dream. A 2000 study found graduation rates to be 76 percent for white students, 57 percent for Native Americans, 55 percent for African Americans, and 53 percent for Hispanics.[6] The newest immigrants look a lot like the oldest "foreigners" in the United States in terms of social status. Unlike whole generations of European immigrants, no amount of assimilation will ever make them white.

Like earlier generations of immigrants, those arriving today still see learning English as crucial to survival and success. But new immigrants also become aware that learning to speak English will not resolve the problems of race. Native Americans and African Americans are native speakers of English—but this has not helped them to assimilate into a U.S. society that still in many ways defines itself as white.

Of all Latino groups in the United States, it's Puerto Ricans who are the most assimilated. All Puerto Ricans have been citizens since 1917. Puerto Ricans tend to know English, and to speak English as their primary language, at much higher rates than other Latinos.[7] Puerto Ricans also have a huge advantage over other immigrants because their citizenship status makes them eligible for public social services and gives them the automatic right to work, rights that many immigrants from other parts of Latin America lack.

Although Mexican nationals are not automatically citizens the way Puerto Ricans are, Mexicans have the longest history in the United States of any Latino group. Mexicans residing in the territories taken by the United States in 1848 were granted citizenship, and Mexicans have been migrating into the United States for a longer time than any other group.

Yet Mexicans and Puerto Ricans have the *highest* poverty rates of any group of Latinos in the United States. Cubans, the vast majority of whom came to the United States after 1959, Dominicans, who started coming in large numbers in the 1970s, and Central Americans, whose massive migration dates to the 1980s, all have much lower poverty rates: 24.1 percent of Mexicans and 23.7 percent of Puerto Ricans in the

United States lived below the poverty line in 2003, while only 14.4 percent of Cubans did.[8]

In an interesting study of black West Indian immigrants, Mary Waters found that "immigrants and their children do better economically by maintaining a strong ethnic identity and culture and by resisting American cultural and identity influences . . . those who resist becoming American do well and those who lose their immigrant ethnic distinctiveness become downwardly mobile . . . When West Indians lose their distinctiveness as immigrants or ethnics they become not just Americans, but black Americans."[9]

The picture is clear. Immigrants of color do assimilate into U.S. society, but, in contrast to white immigrants, for people of color assimilation means downward mobility. Assimilation means learning the racial order of the United States, and for people of color it means joining the lower ranks of that racial order. The association often made between assimilation and upward mobility is based on the experience of white immigrants. For immigrants of color, the trajectory of assimilation is a very different one.

MYTH 13

TODAY'S IMMIGRANTS ARE NOT LEARNING ENGLISH, AND BILINGUAL EDUCATION JUST ADDS TO THE PROBLEM

The long waiting lists for available ESL (English as a Second Language) classes and the overwhelming trend for English to predominate among the second and third generations of immigrants from Latin America belie the common belief that new immigrants are reluctant to learn English. In many ways, the language patterns of today's immigrants are similar to those of earlier generations: older immigrants find learning the new language extremely difficult, and sometimes unnecessary, while the younger generation quickly realizes that English is essential and becomes fluent rapidly. By the third generation, the language of the immigrant's homeland tends to be lost.[1] Often third or fourth generations will study their grandparents' native language in school to try to reconnect with their heritage.

In some ways, though, today's situation is different, and some of these differences have led to misconceptions about what today's immigrants are really doing, especially with respect to learning English.

Many of those who came to the United States from Europe a hundred years ago planned to work hard for a few years and then return to their homelands. Those who carried out this plan rarely learned much English. But for those who ended up staying longer and establishing families here, English came to predominate within a generation or at most two.

This pattern, which prevailed from the 1870s through the early twentieth century, shifted in the decade between 1914 and 1924. The migrant stream was interrupted, in both directions. The First World War and the increasingly restrictive U.S. immigration laws led to a significant reduction in transatlantic travel. This meant that immigrant populations and their cultures ceased to be nourished by a continuing influx, and that immigrants who were here had to give up their hopes of returning home. At the same time, anti-foreign (and especially anti-German) propaganda and Americanization campaigns created further pressures for immigrants to abandon their native languages. Multilingualism came to be replaced by English monolingualism.

Both the past and the present of Latin American immigrants are somewhat different. First, the history of Latin Americans in the United States is one of forcible incorporation as well as immigration. Mexicans and Puerto Ricans were conquered by the United States. Conquered peoples have historically been more marginalized, and more reluctant to give up their cultural heritage, than voluntary immigrants. Many Native American populations, for example, have maintained their languages for hundreds of years after conquest. Likewise, Puerto Ricans resisted the intensive Anglicization campaign that sought to replace Spanish with English on the island in the first half of the twentieth century.

Although the history of conquest and forced incorporation of Spanish-speaking peoples into the United States in some ways structures the experiences of contemporary Latin American immigrants, it's not the only factor that makes their experience different from that of earlier European immigrants. The other major difference is that geography, technology, and immigration patterns keep cross-border ties much more alive for today's Latino immigrants. Their homelands are closer, they can go back and forth more easily and cheaply, they can stay in touch through various electronic media, and immigration is ongoing. So even if second- and third-generation Latinos are speaking English, new first generations are continually rejuvenating the Spanish-speaking population.

From the outside, it may look like Latinos are not learning English. But what's really happening is that as one generation learns English, new Spanish speakers are arriving. At the same time, more Latinos are speaking both languages than has historically been the case for European immigrants. They learn English without giving up Spanish.

In 1980, 11 percent of the U.S. population, or 23.1 million people, spoke a language other than English at home. In 1990, it was 14 percent, or 31.8 million people, and in 2000, it was 18 percent or 47 million people. Over half of these—28.1 million in 2000—were Spanish speakers. (It's worth noting, though, that over half of those who spoke Spanish or another non-English language at home were also proficient in English.)[2] But the pattern of adoption of English has remained consistent: "The longer the length of stay, the more extensive the adoption of the English language."[3] The main variable affecting adoption of English has been age upon arrival: the older the immigrant, the less likely he or she is to become fluent in English.

While it's clear that today's Spanish-speaking immigrants are learning English just as quickly as earlier generations of European immigrants did, they also seem to be retaining their native language at higher levels than did the Europeans. This is probably due to the factors mentioned above: the history of colonization, the geographic proximity, the continuing immigration, and improved communications technology. While over half of third-generation Latino immigrants are monolingual in English, significant numbers are fluent in both English and Spanish.[4]

One way to measure the desire of Latin American immigrants to learn English is through their enrollment in ESL classes. In a recent study, almost 60 percent of ESL providers in the United States reported significant waiting lists —some up to three years. Many of those that reported no waiting list explained that they did not keep a list because there were so many people trying to sign up for their classes, they simply filled the classes then turned people away. In New York City, there were only forty thousand slots for over a million hopeful students.[5]

A study by the Pew Hispanic Foundation asked Latinos

directly how important they believed learning English was. "Hispanics by a large margin believe that immigrants have to speak English to be a part of American society and even more so that English should be taught to the children of immigrants," the authors of the survey concluded. According to the study, 92 percent of Hispanics believed that it was "very important" that the children of immigrants be taught English, compared to 87 percent of non-Hispanic whites and 83 percent of non-Hispanic blacks.[6] Clearly, there is no reluctance to learn English among the Hispanic population.

Why, then, have politicians and activists felt the need to promote "English only" laws and initiatives throughout the United States? By late 2006 twenty-eight states had, through legislation or through the initiative process, declared English as their official language. The organization U.S. English, Inc., founded by former senator S. I. Hayakawa, has been working since 1983 to promote such legislation at the state and national levels. Its goal, the organization announces, is "preserving the unifying role of the English language in the United States."[7] The organization English for the Children has focused its energies on dismantling bilingual education programs, arguing that children should be taught only in English. Led by California businessman Ron Unz, this organization has also succeeded in passing anti-bilingual-education initiatives in California, Arizona, and Massachusetts.[8]

Most supporters of these initiatives argue passionately for the importance of English. But since there is no organized movement in the political or educational spheres, nor any discernable public opinion, that challenges the importance of learning English, the campaign had to find a different target. Instead of targeting immigrants, it targeted the bilingual education programs established in the 1960s to help immigrant children learn English. Ignoring two generations of research on the successes of these programs, Unz and his followers built a campaign on the entirely unsubstantiated notion that bilingual education actually *prevented* children from learning English.

Research on the topic has been fairly unanimous in its conclusions that bilingualism, or multilingualism, offers both cognitive and professional advantages over monolingualism. It also shows that while children can gain conversational knowledge of a new language rather quickly, it takes three to four years for them to develop the academic fluency that allows them to engage in in-depth study in the second language.[9]

Thus children who receive instruction in their native language in subject areas like math, science, and reading while they are learning English consistently show better short-term and long-term results—not only in these subject areas, but also in knowledge of English.[10] These outcomes are unsurprising to cognitive scientists, who have long argued for the benefits of bilingualism.[11]

But the proponents of "English only" ask voters to endorse the proposal that non-English-speaking children's needs will be better met with no instruction in their native language. Rather, they propose a limited period in an ESL classroom, followed by a move into subject areas taught only in English. English-only proponents also raise the specter—also entirely unsupported by any evidence—that bilingualism threatens English.

James Crawford, former president of the National Association of Bilingual Educators, argues that by combining xenophobia with misinformation, the anti-bilingual-education movement has brought both conservatives and liberals into its English-only fold. Some of the leaders of the anti-bilingual movement may be motivated by xenophobia, but most of the voters who have supported the initiatives do so because they have come to believe—contrary to all evidence—that bilingual education disadvantages immigrant children. As Crawford explains, many people vote against bilingual education "in the erroneous belief that it segregates immigrant children, fails to teach them English, and limits their opportunities."[12]

A high-profile—and well-funded—campaign has created this widespread impression that bilingual education impedes children's ability to learn English. According to this theory, learning English and learning other kinds of subject matter are mutually exclusive: either children are taught English, with academic subjects put on hold, or they are isolated in "bilingual" classrooms where they learn their academic subjects in their native language, but no English.

Reagan administration official Linda Chávez "told the stories of children allegedly victimized by a 'multibillion-dollar bureaucracy'—misassigned to bilingual classrooms, held there against their parents' will, and prevented from learning English."[13] Conservative analysts call bilingual education "modern-day segregation... cordoning children into separate classrooms and depriving them of English language skills."[14]

This description fundamentally misconstrues the nature and the goals of bilingual education. Bilingual education is based on the premise that "there is no need to hold children back in English while they learn school subjects in their native language, or to hold them back academically while they acquire English. Quite the contrary. A generation of research and practice has shown that developing academic skills and knowledge in students' vernacular supports their acquisition of English."[15] Most voters, though, don't have the time or the resources to explore the research on language acquisition, and they don't know much about how bilingual programs work.

Furthermore, as Crawford explains, "because bilingual education is controversial, it is reported less as a pedagogical field than a political issue, with opposing 'sides' given equal time."[16] Rather like the issue of evolution, or global warming: there is an overwhelming scientific consensus on the basic issues, but because they are *politically* controversial, they are often presented in the media as if there were equal scientific validity to the opposing political views.

In some ways, the debate about bilingual education mirrors other debates about social policy. Conservatives argue that social spending on programs like welfare, affirmative action, or others designed to address social, racial, and economic inequalities actually harms those whom it is designed to help.

Education should not be understood as a zero-sum issue. Just as children should be taught math *and* reading—and educators understand that literacy enhances math skills, and vice versa—children who are fluent in a language other than English have an academic skill that should be nurtured. Politicians and others who are concerned with immigrants learning English should push for more adult ESL programs, and better funding for bilingual education, rather than punitive measures like English-only ballots and banning the educational programs designed to effectively teach children.

PART FOUR

HOW HAVE U.S. POLICIES CREATED IMMIGRATION?

Discussions of immigration in the news media, in the halls of Congress, or in the streets tend to see immigration as an individual, rather than a structural and historical, issue. They start from the assumption that people in other countries come here to take advantage of the wealth and opportunity that abound in this country. Since waves of immigration are composed of many individual decisions, the argument goes, we need to take steps to stop those individuals once they've made their decisions, otherwise they'll use up all of the wealth and opportunity that by rights should belong first to citizens.

If we look at numbers and trends, however, we can see that migrant flows are in fact highly structured. They're structured by colonial relationships. In fact the current migration streams around the world are one contemporary expression of long-standing, and continuing, social and economic relationships created by colonialism.

There are really two parts of the issue that we need to understand. First, we need to understand why the United

States and other immigrant-receiving countries, like the European countries, are so wealthy. It is not just chance: it has much to do with the colonial world system that emerged after 1492, which drained resources out of Africa, Latin America, and Asia and into the United States and Europe. Given this background, it is little wonder that inhabitants of these former regions want some of the wealth that was created out of their resources and their labor—but that they're denied access to in their homelands.

Second, we need to look at the continuing relationships and ties that make immigration a possibility and a reality. Disparities in resources don't, on their own, lead to immigration. It's the economic ties created by colonial and neocolonial economies, economic demand in the receiving country, and even, in many cases, direct recruitment that set the stage for immigration.

MYTH 14

IMMIGRANTS ONLY COME HERE BECAUSE THEY WANT TO ENJOY OUR HIGHER STANDARD OF LIVING

Immigrants do come to the United States because the standard of living is so much higher here than in their own countries. But that's not the whole story. The main countries from which people migrate to the United States are not the poorest countries of the world, and the people who migrate are not the poorest people. In fact the poorest countries—most of which are in Africa—send only tiny numbers of migrants to the United States. Puerto Rico, by far the wealthiest area in Latin America, has sent almost half of its population to the United States, while Bolivia, one of the poorest countries, has sent hardly any migrants. The largest number of migrants comes from Mexico—which is one of the wealthier countries of Latin America.[1]

Every immigrant comes for individual reasons. But patterns of immigration have structural and historical causes. There is not one single cause that explains all immigration. There are, though, several major interrelated factors that have structured immigration in the past and that continue to structure it today.

Immigrants usually explain their decision to leave their home country for another in terms of push–pull factors. Poverty, lack of opportunity, and danger "push" people to leave; opportunity, availability of jobs, education, and safety "pull" people elsewhere. Still, these well-known explanations don't really explain very much. They fail to explain just why some places seem to be characterized by poverty, lack of opportunity, and danger while others offer opportunity, jobs, education, and safety. They also don't explain why long-standing inequalities among regions or countries lead only sometimes to flows of migration.

The more sophisticated explanations look at patterns. A closer look at some specific cases, with particular attention to Puerto Rico and the Philippines, reveals some of the factors that structured twentieth-century migrations. Of course Puerto Ricans have been U.S. citizens since 1917, so when we talk about Puerto Rico we are not talking about international migration. But the patterns of Puerto Rican migration to the continental United States shed light on what is going on elsewhere too.

Puerto Ricans are not the largest group of Latin Americans in the continental United States numerically, but Puerto Rico has sent a greater proportion of its population to the U.S. than any other country. Some 40 percent of Puerto Ricans have left the island for the continent. So it's an excellent place to begin investigating the question of why people migrate.

As is the case for most migrant flows, the sending and the receiving countries—in this case the United States and Puerto Rico—have a long-standing relationship. The United States took Puerto Rico from Spain in 1898 as part of the spoils of the Spanish-American War and ruled it as a colony until 1952. Globally, this kind of long-standing relationship is an important one to look at in understanding migration. People from India and Pakistan go to England; people from Senegal and Algeria go to France; people from Morocco go to Spain; people from Mexico and Puerto Rico come to the United States. *Colonization sets the stage for later migration.* This is why Juan González called his book on Latinos in the United States *The Harvest of Empire*—because empire spawns migration.

Colonization creates cultural ties. It brings people from the metropolis (the colonizing power) to the colony and places them in positions of power while destroying local institutions. (Puerto Rico offers something of a variation on the general pattern here, since it was already a colony when the United States took over, rather than being self-governing.) Colonization almost always brings in structures of cultural and racial inequality, imbuing the institutions of the colony with the idea of the "white man's burden"—the idea that white Europeans are culturally superior. In this respect, Puerto Rico's experience is typical.

U.S. cultural imperialism in Puerto Rico took the form of an Anglicization campaign. The name of the island was officially changed to "Porto Rico." The U.S. commissioner of education explained in 1903 that "their language is a patois almost unintelligible to the natives of Barcelona or Madrid. It possesses no literature and has little value as an intellectual medium. There is a bare possibility that it will be nearly as easy to educate this people out of their patois into English as it will be to educate them into the elegant tongue of Castile."[2] English, then, was introduced as the language of the educational system.

Magali García Ramis's novel *Happy Days, Uncle Sergio* gives some poignant examples of how cultural imperialism works. She describes growing up in a middle-class family on the island in the 1950s with Puerto Rican culture and identity being systematically erased and denied.

"There are no famous Puerto Rican artists because Puerto Rico doesn't have much culture and this island is too small," the narrator Lidia's brother explains to her. "Only now as part of the U.S., as a Commonwealth, has Puerto Rico begun to progress."[3] Americans, the children are constantly told, "had to be admired and loved more than any other people, because they were good. They had saved the world from the Nazis, and now they were protecting it from the Communists. Also they were geniuses when it came to technology and progress. The dam we had just visited had been designed by Americans along with a few Puerto Ricans who studied in the United States."[4]

As a teenager, Lidia despairs.

> Why don't we have anything of value, Uncle? Why don't we have a single worldwide famous artist, a poet, a painter? . . . In the series *Exemplary Lives* they've pre-

> sented dozens of famous people from all over the world, from India, Argentina, the United States, Sweden, France, and never one from Puerto Rico. On dictionary flaps they put the flags of all the countries, even one of the International Red Cross, those of the British Colonies, and the Virgin Islands, but ours is never there, because we aren't anything, not a country or a colony or a commonwealth like the British islands. We're nothing. We don't exist. We are shit, I thought, and I don't want to belong to this country![5]

A Filipina nurse, one of thousands who came to work in U.S. hospitals, expressed a similar sentiment. "The thing I love about American hospitals is that we have enough supplies and equipment. You have catheters . . . In the Philippines we boiled our own rectal tubes. You use the catheters over and over. . . Here you just use it once and dump it out. Supplies and equipment, paper, everything. It was no comparison. [In the Philippines], it was so limited all the time."[6] New York City hospitals trying to recruit Filipina nurses projected a similarly glorified image. "We will help you cross the BRIDGE from where you are to where you want to be . . . NEW YORK CITY! No matter where you are—your nursing diploma can bring you to New York City. . . Imagine! Living and working in America's most exciting city. . . where the whole world looks for the finest medical care!"[7]

Lidia's lament, like that of the Filipina nurse, reveals what some have termed a "colonized mentality." The colonial power projects an image of omnipotence and superiority and reiterates the inferiority of those it has colonized. Is it any surprise that colonial subjects dream of leaving home for the metropolis?

It's not only in Puerto Rico that the United States has successfully projected its image of wealth and omnipotence. Many Latin Americans refer to the current relationship of their countries to the United States as a *neocolonial* relationship. Although the United States does not directly govern their countries, it exerts economic, political, and military control through indirect means.

U.S. military bases and troops span the globe. Since the 1950s, some 500,000 U.S. troops have been deployed around the world, many without permission and without visas from the countries that they go to, making them, essentially, illegal immigrants.[8] In Honduras in the 1980s, some officials coined the nickname "USS Honduras," referring to the overwhelming U.S. military presence there.[9] According to Chalmers Johnson, this "vast network of American bases on every continent except Antarctica actually constitutes a new form of empire"—an "empire of bases."[10]

The lure of the United States as the source of superabundance and wealth is also projected worldwide through film, radio, and television. The film *El Norte* depicts how images of the United States permeate a remote village in Guatemala's indigenous highlands, through copies of *Good Housekeeping* that a woman there received from a friend who was a maid in the house of an American in the capital. "Everybody there has a flush toilet!" she proclaims.

Immigrants to the United States perpetuate the image, sometimes deliberately, sometimes in spite of themselves. When friends and relatives sacrifice to send someone to the United States, the immigrant bears a heavy obligation to repay the debt. Anthropologist Sarah Mahler describes how Salvadorans on Long Island respond to the guilt and obligation they feel by sending home exaggerated accounts of their success. Another anthropologist, Roger Lancaster, describes the importance of dollars to poor Nicaraguans.[11]

U.S. tourists, sometimes in spite of themselves, also contribute. After a ten-day study-travel stay in Cuba, one of my U.S. students wrote, "I often found myself . . . attempting to convince them of the existence of a large, economically marginalized portion of the United States. Yet no matter what I told them the fact was that I stood before them as someone who had traveled outside of her own country, with my fancy camera, new sneakers, having never experienced a blackout, or a shortage of water, let alone being hungry. In this respect, I was just more proof of the U.S.'s opulence."[12]

With 4 percent of the world's population, the United States consumes 22 percent of its electricity, 25 percent of its oil, and 23 percent of its natural gas.[13] It's not surprising that people in other countries are taken aback at our level of consumption—especially if they're the ones producing what we're consuming.

Colonization also brought about economic transformations in the colonies that contribute to migration and, in particular, migration to the metropolis. In the industrial era (starting in the middle of the nineteenth century), the colonial powers used their colonies as a source of raw materials, and as a market for their manufactured goods. Colonies provided agricultural products like sugar, coffee, tea, bananas, and tobacco, all of which made it cheap to feed the industrial working class at home, and they provided raw materials for industry, like tin and copper.

To produce these raw materials, companies and governments had to find a way to entice or force colonized peoples away from subsistence farms and villages to work in plantations and mines. Labor recruiters used varying levels of coercion to obtain workers. Sometimes they lent money, or made false promises. Sometimes, villages were destroyed when plantations or mines took over or contaminated the land. (See the epilogue for a description of a contemporary example of this process.)

Whether forced or voluntary, the move from subsistence production to wage labor brought about fundamental changes in social organization. People who had formerly produced most of what they consumed now produced for others and used their wages to consume goods imported from the metropolis. Often, people left their villages to migrate to plantations or urban centers for work. Once traditional village life and ties are unraveled, migration out of the country becomes a real possibility.

Foreign-owned corporations, like armies, tourists, and military bases, tend to bring a small part of the First World into the midst of the Third. Consider the contrast between the Tintaya copper mine and the rest of the country of Peru, in which it operates, as described by Dan Baum in *The New Yorker*:

> Peru's per-capita gross domestic product is less than that of Namibia or the Dominican Republic, but the Anglo-Australian Tintaya copper mine is a decidedly First World operation. The man-made canyon of the open pit is bordered by a spotless miniature city—neat workers' houses with flowers out front, garden apartments, a chapel, a hotel, a hospital, a health club, and office buildings. The rules of conduct are enforced with the rigor of a military academy: no walking in the street, no crossing outside the zebra stripes, no smoking, and orange vests and hard hats required everywhere. The mine's obsessive rectitude, amid the nearly uninhabited high grassy plains and snow-capped mountains of southeastern Peru, is as anomalous as a moon colony in a science-fiction story. Engineers at Tintaya work in cubicles, each with a late-model I.B.M. ThinkPad attached to a nineteen-inch L.C.D. monitor, their whiteboards covered with dizzying graphs, parabolas, and complicated equations.

It's not surprising that Peruvians employed by the mine start to think about emigration. The *New Yorker* profile of one immigrant explained, "Though happy in his job, Raúl yearned for a life as orderly as the mine, for a country that funded education and parks, regulated air pollution and noise, and policed its own lawmakers."[14]

From the mid-nineteenth century on, Puerto Ricans produced sugar and coffee for U.S. markets and imported U.S manufactured goods. Many migrated from rural to urban areas. As early as the 1920s, U.S. manufacturers began to experiment with shipping parts of their production to Puerto Rico. Puerto Rican women, in factories and in their homes, sewed and embroidered handkerchiefs and clothing that went back to U.S. markets.

The colonial relationship invariably drains resources from the colony to the metropolis. Colonial subjects see their homeland deteriorate and the colonial power expand its wealth and power. The lure is inescapable.

But Puerto Rico was a U.S. colony, and it was poor and lacking in opportunity (like most other colonies), for a long time before the large flow of Puerto Ricans into the continental United States started. Two interrelated things happened in the 1940s that turned the long-standing unequal relationship into a cause for mass migration.

One side of the coin was Operation Bootstrap (which I discuss in more depth in Part One). U.S. investment had been streaming into Puerto Rico for decades, but Operation Bootstrap was something new. Up until now colonial powers had used their colonies to support industrialization at home. Now a colonial power began to take advantage of colonial labor to *deindustrialize* at home.

The other side was recruitment. Puerto Ricans were recruited to fill wartime shortages of agricultural workers in the U.S. northeast. Increasingly, though, they were also recruited by low-wage industries on the continent that were trying to compete with those that were beginning to move abroad—especially New York's garment industries. As the global economy created greater opportunities for profit, businesses took them, any way they could.

The migration of Puerto Ricans to the mainland, then, was a result not just of the fact that the United States was wealthier and offered higher wages than Puerto Rico. It was the dynamic relationship between the two that put into progress the process of migration. Until Puerto Ricans were fully removed from a subsistence economy, higher wages were not an important draw. Until recruiters came to the island, and until people began working for U.S.-owned factories on the island, the possibility of moving to the mainland to work in a U.S. factory didn't become a reality.

Again, García Ramis captures in her novel the cultural and economic threads that Operation Bootstrap wove, leading to migration. "It was a time of hope that still smelled like new. It was a time of razing red clay mountains to build houses in suburbs, of dissecting every green mountain with asphalt roads, of blossoming cement and hotels, of inaugurating dams and electric power stations, and of waiting in the new airport, that one day would be international, for the arrival of Americans dressed in iridescent gray suits."[15]

As Douglas Massey explains in the case of Mexico,

> That Mexico is by far the largest source of U.S. immigrants is hardly surprising. In addition to sharing a land border with the United States, it was twice invaded by U.S. troops in the 20th century (in 1914 and 1917), it has been the target of two U.S.-sponsored labor recruitment efforts (during 1917–18 and 1942–64), and since 1986, at U.S. insistence, it has undertaken a radical transformation of its political economy and entered the global market. Moreover, since 1994 it has been linked to the United States by NAFTA, a comprehensive economic treaty that presently generates $250 billion per year in binational trade. Under these circumstances, immigration between the two countries is inevitable, even though Mexico is wealthy by Third World standards.[16]

When people raise the question of "why do people migrate?" it's often because they consider migration to be a negative thing, and they want to know how to stop it. The explanation proposed here doesn't mean to imply a judgment about migration. What it tries to do is to place migration in a historical context, and see it as part of a larger global system. Citizen workers who have lost their jobs to global restructuring and migrants who have come to the United States to fill the new secondary labor market are part of a system that is much larger than themselves. Migration is a result, not a cause, of these global economic changes.

CASE STUDY

THE PHILIPPINES

Puerto Rico and the Philippines are two of the areas that have sent the greatest proportion of their populations to the United States. The parallels in their histories can help to explain why.

Puerto Rico, with almost 3 million migrants, and the Philippines, with almost 1.5 million migrants, represent, after Mexico and China (both much larger countries), the largest migrant groups in the United States. (Mexico had over 9 million, according to the 2000 census, and China 1.5 million.) The 2000 census surveys recorded a total population of 76 million in the Philippines and 3.8 million in Puerto Rico.

Like Puerto Rico, the Philippines was a Spanish colony coveted by the United States until 1898. "Cuba has a remarkable counterpart in the Far East," explained the U.S. minister to Siam in 1897. The natives are "gentle, polite, and hospitable," yet not at all "ambitious": "thirty-five dollars will provide a man with abundant food and clothing for a year." Furthermore, "although inclined to be lazy, as are all tropical people, they are exceedingly fond of amusements."[17]

The people may have been poor, but the land was rich. "In

material wealth the Philippines are lavishly blessed. Hemp, sugar, and tobacco are three products that bring enormous profits, and coffee bids fair to soon rival them." Foreign trade was valued at $35 million the previous year.[18] "The prodigality of nature impresses the traveler wherever he journeys."[19]

Almost everybody in the United States has heard of the "Spanish-American War." This war was fought, of course, in Cuba, and Cubans tend to see it as just one more example of imperial arrogance that their role in the war is ignored in the United States. Actually, the Cubans had been fighting for several decades for independence from Spain before the United States intervened in 1898.

The Treaty of Paris that ended the war ceded not only Cuba but also other formerly Spanish island territories to the United States: Puerto Rico, Guam, and the Philippines. The first three acquiesced relatively peacefully to the transfer of power from Spain to the United States, but the Philippine independence movement rose up in arms. The U.S.–Philippine war hasn't entered the history books —it doesn't even have an official name. But it was the first guerrilla war, and the first Asian war, that the United States fought. More people died in that conflict than in the Spanish-American War, and it lasted much longer.

In the context of the U.S. war against the Philippines, Rudyard Kipling published his well-known poem "The White Man's Burden," defending the colonial enterprise, in *McClure's Magazine* in February 1899. The "burden" was the racial obligation to conquer—for the benefit of the Filipinos, of course: "Send forth the best ye breed," Kipling wrote, "Go bind your sons to exile, / To serve your captives' need." Those conquered were notoriously ungrateful for the sacrifice the whites made on their behalf: the "new-caught, sullen peoples, / Half-devil and half-child" usually gave the white man only his "old reward": "the blame of those ye better, / The hate of those ye guard." Still, his inherent superiority gave the white man the duty to govern others, even against their will.[20]

One outspoken southern challenger of the U.S. racial order at the time, Reverend Quincy Ewing of Mississippi, noted the connection between domestic racism and foreign expansion inherent in the poem:

> Northern applause of the policy of shooting down weaker brown men in distant islands to civilize them, or even to "save their souls"—must inevitably plant seeds of bitter fruit for black men in the southern states of this country, and perhaps, nay, very probably, in all the others. I cannot believe I am mistaken in supposing that the lynching spirit has shown itself conspicuously bold and self-congratulatory in the northern and western as well as in the southern states of the union, since it became possible for the hoarse and brutal muse of Rudyard Kipling to sing the nation's policy and purpose. If millions of brown men across the thousands of miles of sea are the white nation's burden—to be dealt with as a burden—why may not the white men of the southern states look upon the

> black man, separated from them by no sea at all, as their burden, to be dealt with as a burden rather than as men?[21]

Political cartoons consistently used racist images based on blacks in the U.S. south to depict the inhabitants of Cuba, Puerto Rico, and the Philippines. American soldiers "commonly referred to Filipinos as 'niggers.' "[22]

As Senator Alfred Beveridge proclaimed in 1898, "Why is it more difficult to administer Hawaii than New Mexico or California? Both had a savage and an alien population: both were more remote from the seat of government when they came under our dominion than the Philippines are today." Colonial subjects were to be ruled. To opponents who questioned the legitimacy of Anglo-Saxon rule over others, he replied, "We govern the Indians without their consent, we govern our territories without their consent."[23]

Others used the association of old and new colonial subjects to argue against annexation. Southern segregationists like Benjamin Tillman could also be anti-imperialists. Tillman referred to Kipling's poem when he explained to the U.S. Senate in 1899 why southern Democrats had voted overwhelmingly against the treaty:

> It was not because we are Democrats, but because we understand and realize what it is to have two races side by side that can not mix or mingle without deterioration and injury to both and the ultimate destruction of the civilization of the higher. We of the South have

> borne this white man's burden of a colored race in our midst since their emancipation and before.
>
> It was a burden upon our manhood and our ideas of liberty before they were emancipated. It is still a burden, although they have been granted the franchise . . . We are not responsible, because we inherited it, and your fathers as well as ours are responsible for the presence amongst us of that people. Why do we as a people want to incorporate into our citizenship ten millions more of different or of differing races, three or four of them?[24]

Still, as journalist and diplomat John Barrett pointed out in the *North American Review*, the Philippines were "one of the greatest undeveloped opportunities in all the world—a group of islands with numberless riches and resources awaiting exploitation, and capable of providing a market for a large quantity of our manufactured products."[25]

Until 1898, all of the territories that the United States incorporated fell under the Northwest Ordinance of 1787—they were incorporated with the understanding that they would ultimately be admitted into statehood. The size of the nonwhite populations of Cuba, Puerto Rico, and the Philippines worried even the most ardent imperialists. In 1901, the Supreme Court resolved the issue by creating the category of "unincorporated territory" that allowed the United States to own and control the territories without having to extend the Constitution to them. "Whilst in an international sense Porto Rico was not a foreign country, since it was subject to the sovereignty of and was owned by the United States, it was foreign to the United States in a domestic sense," explained the court.[26]

"We come not as invaders or conquerors, but as friends," President McKinley explained in announcing U.S. sovereignty in the Philippines. He declared that all who cooperated "will receive the reward of [U.S.] support and protection. All others will be brought within the lawful rule we have assumed, with firmness if need be."[27]

Likewise in a proclamation to the people of Puerto Rico upon occupying their country in July 1898, U.S. general Nelson Miles insisted upon the benevolence of his enterprise:

> In the cause of liberty, justice, and humanity, [U.S.] military forces have come to occupy the island of Puerto Rico. They come bearing the banner of freedom, inspired by a noble purpose to seek the enemies of our country and yours, and to destroy or capture all who are in armed resistance . . . The chief object of the American military forces will be to overthrow the armed authority of Spain, and to give the people of your beautiful island the largest measure of liberty consistent with this occupation . . . It is not our purpose to interfere with any existing laws and customs . . . so long as they conform to the rules of military administration of order and justice. This is not a war of devastation, but one to give all within the control of [U.S.] military and naval forces the advantages and blessings of enlightened civilization.[28]

For the people of these territories, too, a new category had to be invented: the "U.S. national," neither citizen nor alien. They had no political rights, but they did have the right to travel to the mainland.[29] Some protested that Filipinos, because they were racially ineligible for citizenship, should be excluded under the same laws that prohibited other Asians from entering the United States. Congress, however, insisted that the United States could not prohibit entry as long as it held the Philippines as a territory.

Sugar plantations in Hawaii recruited and imported both Puerto Rican and Filipino workers, taking advantage of their status as "nationals." U.S. sugar planters in Hawaii had imported over 200,000 workers from Japan, China, Portugal, and Puerto Rico in the late nineteenth century, before the islands were subject to U.S. immigration laws. When Hawaii was annexed in 1898, however, planters turned to the Philippines. From 1909 to 1929, some 120,000 Filipinos were brought to Hawaii to work on the plantations.[30] Many of those followed labor recruiters on to the mainland, to the fields of California. The 1930 census found 45,000 Filipinos on the mainland and 63,000 in Hawaii.[31]

Lawyer Madison Grant, one of the founders of the U.S. eugenicist and "scientific" racist movement in the early twentieth century (and cited as an inspiration for Nazi eugenics policy), wrote, "The swarming of the Filipinos into the Pacific states brings with it a repetition of the Chinese problem of sixty years ago. California is determined that the white man there shall not be replaced by the Chinese, the Japanese, the Mexican, or the Filipino."[32] In the view of the scientific racists, the white man's destiny was to "replace" people of color, but never to be "replaced" by them. Perhaps at the heart of these manifestations of racial exclusionism in the United States is the original sin—the fact that the country was founded, and expanded, by replacing its original inhabitants. In order to justify this original replacement, the right of whites to expand, and the fate of people of color to disappear, had to be constantly reiterated and reenacted.

In 1934 the Philippines Independence Act turned the country into a commonwealth—another invented status—and putting it on a ten-year path to independence.[33] Echoing Samuel Gompers's argument against annexation of the Philippines three decades earlier, Madison Grant wrote that "as a safeguard to our own racial welfare, it might become necessary to give the Filipino his independence."[34]

With the stroke of a pen, Filipinos became "aliens" and lost their right to enter the United States. U.S. citizens retained *their* right to enter the Philippines and be treated as full citizens there.[35] The 60,000 Filipinos who had settled in the United States, mostly as agricultural workers in California, were offered various incentives for repatriation. Few were interested in the offer, especially since it meant giving up their right to return to the United States.

California's nineteenth-century anti-miscegenation laws prohibited marriages between whites and "negroes, mulattoes, and Mongolians."[36] Such legislation was upheld by the U.S. Supreme Court in 1883, and by the 1920s thirty-eight states had anti-miscegenation laws on the books. Sixteen states still prohibited interracial marriage when the court overturned that ruling in 1967. (Alabama did not revoke its statute until 2000, and even then, 40 percent of the voters wanted to keep it.)[37]

The courts could not agree, however, on whether Filipinos were "Mongolians" or "Malays," and in 1933 the Los Angeles Superior Court allowed a Filipino man to marry a white woman—at the same time urging the state legislature to amend the law so that Filipinos would be included. The legislature did so later that year, including "members of the Malay race" among those prohibited from marrying Caucasians.[38]

"The dominant race of the country has a perfect right to exclude all other races from equal rights with its own people," explained the presiding judge in one case in the late 1920s that ruled against the right of a Filipino to marry a Caucasian.[39] "I am quite satisfied in my own mind," wrote another judge in another 1930s California case, "that the Filipino is a Malay and that a Malay is a Mongolian, just as much as the white American is of the Teutonic race, the Teutonic family, or of the Nordic family, carrying it back to the Aryan family. Hence, it is my view that under the Code of California as it now exists, intermarriage between a Filipino and a Caucasian would be void."[40]

Even as the doors of exclusion were closing on Filipinos, the seeds for a later migration were being sown through the U.S. colonial system in the Philippines. Establishing a public health and sanitation infrastructure was a component of U.S. imperial policy in both the Caribbean and the Pacific. It supported the ideology of Anglo-Saxon uplift of backward peoples and conveniently made the tropics safe for white settlers at the same time.[41] During the 1920s the U.S. government and the Rockefeller Foundation International Health Board created a nursing education program in the Philippines based on the U.S. model. The language of instruction was English.

When Filipino independence was finally completed in 1946 (delayed by the Second World War), it was qualified by the Bell Act, which stipulated an unequal "free trade"—U.S. goods could enter the Philippines in unlimited quantities, duty free, while Filipino goods were subject to quotas. U.S. citizens and corporations were also granted investment privileges in the country. Finally, the U.S. controlled the exchange rate. In addition, the U.S. maintained full sovereignty over its twenty-three military installations in the Philippines.[42]

Filipinos had, of course, been working for U.S. employers for years: on sugar plantations, as soldiers in the U.S. army, and on U.S. bases in the Philippines, which directly employed almost 70,000 Filipinos in the 1980s.[43] Independence only reinforced the unequal economic and cultural relationships that contributed to migration.

A generation of Filipina nurses was poised to take advantage of the opportunity created in 1948 when the U.S. began an exchange visitor program to bring Filipina nurses to the U.S. for postgraduate study in U.S. hospitals.[44] Airlines and travel agencies enthusiastically promoted the program in the Philippines.[45]

The ostensible idea of the program was that the nurses

would return home to bring their education back to their people. But in the United States, a nursing shortage approaching crisis proportions led hospitals to recruit the students and provide them with green cards to stay and work here. Between 1948 and 1973, 12,000 Filipina nurses came to the States to study, and many of them stayed and became citizens.[46] The 1965 Immigration Act added incentives by making nurses a category of workers eligible for preferential visas, and U.S. hospitals and Filipino travel agencies stepped up their recruitment efforts.[47] (Another 17,000 Filipinos were brought to the U.S. for military training between 1950 and the early 1980s.[48] By 1970, 14,000 Filipinos were serving in the U.S. navy, more than the total number serving in the Philippines' own navy.[49]) By 1989, 73 percent of foreign nurses in the United States were from the Philippines. They worked primarily in large public hospitals in major U.S. cities. In New York City, 18 percent of RNs were Filipino.[50]

By 2005, U.S. hospitals were reporting an ever-growing nursing deficit that had reached 118,000.[51] The "nursing shortage" in the United States was rooted in two interrelated phenomena. First, low wages and poor working conditions are characteristic of nursing jobs, as they are of agricultural and domestic work. Not surprisingly, people with other options tend to avoid the most onerous ones. Employers then find that they can't fill their positions, and the government helps them to import workers who have fewer options.

Second, the health-care sector underwent its own restructuring in the post-1965 period. U.S. workers began to obtain health plans through their employers even prior to 1965. Government programs like Medicare and Medicaid increased access to health care in the 1960s. The shift from private doctors to HMOs and hospitals in the 1980s and '90s further increased the demand for nurses. Government cutbacks and employer pressure, meanwhile, forced health-care providers to continually cut costs. So the demand for nurses rose, but working conditions in the sector stayed poor.[52]

As with agriculture, the U.S. government has greatly facilitated a continuing influx of foreign nurses. Some qualify for immigrant visas because the Department of Labor has kept nurses listed as a profession in need of immigrant workers; others come on temporary work visas. Repeated revisions of the law have allowed more nurses to come, and made it easier for them to stay.[53] The American Hospital Association began recruiting heavily abroad, especially in the Philippines, but also in China and India. In 2005, Congress authorized an additional 50,000 visas for nurses because the 12,000 to 14,000 already authorized were nowhere near enough to fill the demand.[54]

Even with the poor conditions in the nursing field, as the labor market in the U.S. got worse overall, more citizens began to turn to nursing as a potential career. Nursing school applications skyrocketed. By 2005, U.S. nursing schools were rejecting 150,000 qualified applicants a year because they didn't have enough spaces. And they couldn't expand, because *teaching* nursing paid even less than *being* a nurse. With the shortages, schools couldn't attract teachers.[55]

The United States wasn't the only wealthy country facing the "care deficit" described by Arlie Hochschild and Barbara Ehrenreich (see Myth 2, on immigrants and low-paying jobs). The preparation of nurses for service abroad became a major industry in the Philippines. By 2000, over 150,000 Filipina nurses were employed in the United Kingdom, Canada, Australia, New Zealand, and the Middle East.[56]

As the U.S. Congress debated new immigration legislation in 2006, the American Hospital Association lobbied hard for unlimited entry of foreign nurses. The Senate bill included this provision, though the House bill did not.[57]

For the Philippines and other poor countries, the hemorrhage of nurses to the wealthy world had contradictory effects. Starting salary for a nurse in the Philippines is about $2,000 a year, while in the United States it's around $36,000.[58] Filipinos working abroad sent back $10.7 billion in remittances in 2005, 13.5 percent of the country's GDP.[59]

On the other hand, as the *New York Times* explained, "Health care has deteriorated there in recent years as tens of thousands of nurses have moved abroad. Thousands of ill-paid doctors have even abandoned their profession to become migrant-ready nurses themselves, Filipino researchers say. 'The Filipino people will suffer because the U.S. will get all our trained nurses,' said George Cordero, president of the Philippine Nurse Association. 'But what can we do?' " A former director of the Philippine National Institutes of Health estimated that 80 percent of the country's doctors had moved, or were in the process of moving, into nursing. "I plead for justice," he told the *Times*. "There has to be give and take, not just take, take, take by the United States."[60]

The specific events described here help to explain why the Philippines, like Puerto Rico, sends such an extraordinarily high proportion of its population to the United States. They also reveal a larger pattern. Colonialism sets up a system in which colonized peoples work for those who colonized them. This system is not erased after direct colonialism ends. Rather, it evolves and develops. The colonizer continues to use former colonial subjects as cheap workers, and the unequal economic relationship is also reinforced in this way. Immigration is just one piece of this larger puzzle, interlocking with all of the other pieces.

PART FIVE
THE DEBATE AT THE TURN OF THE MILLENNIUM

The immigration debate has become increasingly acrimonious in the first years of the new millennium. Pundits and politicians demand a solution to the immigration "crisis." The more they talk about the crisis, the more worried people seem to become about it. With so many well-placed voices talking about a crisis, people begin to feel there really is one.

We need to pause, though, and think about what exactly is so dangerous about immigration—what makes it a crisis.

For many Americans, there is indeed a crisis. It's a crisis of worsening jobs and working conditions, of deterioration of public services, of lack of health insurance. It's an economic crisis. It's also a crisis that benefits one sector of society: the very rich. And it's a crisis that has very little to do with immigration.

There's also another crisis facing many Americans, and that's the crisis of national security. Americans are being sent to fight in far-off wars, and like Rudyard Kipling's "new-caught, sullen peoples," people in Iraq and Afghanistan don't seem properly grateful for American troops' sacrifices. Instead, the people we've invaded seem intent on driving out or killing their presumed saviors. Meanwhile, anger at the United States and its policies, and threats of attack against this country, are increasing.

Then there's the crisis of global warming, and scientists' predictions that if we keep up our current rate of consumption, our common homeland, the earth, will become uninhabitable in the foreseeable future.

With so many real crises facing us, why has so much national attention been focused instead on the issue of immigration? Perhaps the pundits and politicians who are spending so much energy whipping up this immigration scare are trying to distract us from some other, more pressing, national—and global—issues.

MYTH 15

THE AMERICAN PUBLIC OPPOSES IMMIGRATION, AND THE DEBATE IN CONGRESS REFLECTS THAT

First, we should remember that Democrats and Republicans within the U.S. mainstream share a broad set of values and beliefs. In the global spectrum, they fall pretty close together. Both Democrats and Republicans have supported and helped to orchestrate the global and domestic economic order that has emerged since the 1970s. In broad terms, this has meant privatizations, a shift away from government regulation of industry, cutbacks in government services, and a free trade agenda that has pushed other governments—especially Third World governments—to follow these same policies in more extreme ways.

Domestically, this process has been described as a retreat from the mid-century redistributive government role embodied in the New Deal and the War on Poverty. Although those programs are associated (rightly) with the Democratic Party, the Democrats of the late twentieth and early twenty-first centuries have retreated from the social welfare orientation of their predecessors, at least at the national level.

Internationally, the new consensus is sometimes (not very accurately) called globalization. The philosophy behind it can be seen in the Chicago School of Economics–inspired program implemented in Chile in the 1970s, in the Structural Adjustment Programs (or SAPs) mandated by the World Bank and the International Monetary Fund for the Third World in the 1980s, and in the so-called Washington Consensus prescribed for Latin American and other Third World economies in the 1990s.

Though they have different names, these policy approaches all encompass similar basic principles, sometimes also called "neoliberal" because they draw on some aspects of nineteenth-century liberal economic thought (which is very different from what Americans generally think of as "liberal" in the twentieth century). They call for cutting back government spending on social welfare (including health and education), encouraging the export economy by devaluing currency and ending currency controls and tariffs, eliminating government subsidies for programs for the poor, abolishing price controls, privatizing state-owned enterprises, creating incentives for foreign investors, deregulating industries, and protecting property rights.

In other words, the role of governments in the Third World should be to create optimum conditions for foreign investors, in hopes that investment will bring economic development that will eventually benefit the poor. In the United States these kinds of policies are often called "Reaganomics," after Ronald Reagan, or "trickle-down economics": by offering the rich greater ability to increase their wealth, benefits will eventually trickle down to the poor.

Prior to the 1970s, most Latin American countries had followed a very different economic path, one that looked a bit more like the New Deal. The mid-century policies were different from the New Deal because Latin American countries in general had a low level of industrialization, and a lot of emphasis was placed on state-sponsored industrialization. But they were similar to the New Deal in their use of government spending to provide services and employment for the working classes, and implementation of fiscal policies aimed at supporting local development rather than foreign investment.

The most recent embodiments of the neoliberal model have been the free trade agreements that the United States signed with Mexico and Canada in 1994 and those that are currently in progress (agreed upon and approved by the United States, but awaiting final approval by some of the participants) with the Dominican Republic and Central America: NAFTA and CAFTA. The United States has also been pushing for the Free Trade Area of the Americas, which would spread this agenda through the entire continent. Since 2000, though, the election of leftist governments in Venezuela, Brazil, Argentina, Chile, and Bolivia has derailed the push for the FTAA.

Neoliberal policies have had profound effects on the populations and social structures of Latin American countries. Living conditions for the poor, who relied on subsidized services and basic goods and on price controls, plummeted as the safety net was dismantled. Free trade was also disastrous for many peasant farmers, who could not compete with the highly mechanized and heavily subsidized U.S. agricultural sector whose products then flooded their country's markets. While U.S. economic advisers and lenders insisted that Latin American countries end their subsidies to the agricultural sector, U.S. agribusiness continued to receive huge subsidies and benefits from the U.S. government.

Peasants who fled to the already overcrowded cities found the social services and benefits there vanishing. The new maquiladora industries employed some people, but far fewer than had been expected, and often they did not pay a living wage. In addition, popular protest often met with increasing repression. Free-market policies may be associated with democracy in the United States and elsewhere in the industrialized world, but in the Third World, they more commonly come with the disappearance of democratic rights, as in Pinochet's Chile.

This is the complex of factors—pressed for by both Democratic and Republican administrations—that led to increased out-migration from Latin America at the end of the twentieth century. At the same time, though, both Democratic and Republic administrations were implementing a U.S. version of neoliberalism at home. Welfare reform, privatizations, cutbacks in social services like health and education, attacks on labor unions, deregulation—all of these things were happening in the United States as well, and contributing to the growing gaps in income and wealth in this country.

Despite these broad areas of agreement, policymakers, commentators, and the public at large can often be found hotly debating the issue of immigration. Within the mainstream, the current debate on immigration can be framed by the recent Senate and House bills that propose solutions to the supposed problem of immigration. There are some significant differences between the bills, but there are also some important commonalities. The 2006 Senate bill, known as the Kennedy-McCain proposal, has been called a "comprehensive" proposal because it provides a path for the 11 million undocumented immigrants already in the country to obtain legal status. In addition, it provides for increased border control and a guest-worker program to regulate future immigration. The House bill is an "enforcement-only" approach that puts much more emphasis on border control: it proposes building a new seven-hundred-mile wall along the southern border, hiring ten thousand new Border Patrol agents, building new detention facilities, and further criminalizing undocumented immigrants and those who employ or aid them.

The Senate bill is the more liberal of the two and enjoys support from a number of liberal advocacy groups—but also from President Bush. Most of its backers are Democrats, though significant numbers of Republicans also support it. The House bill is a Republican-sponsored bill that only small numbers of Democrats have come out in favor of.

Most immigrants' rights groups argue strongly for the

need for a comprehensive reform. Some have come out in support of the Senate bill, believing that it is the best that can be hoped for in the current political climate.[1] Others object to the punitive requirements for legalization, and to the notion of a new guest-worker program.[2] Unions are similarly divided. The AFL-CIO opposes the Senate plan, arguing that guest-worker programs by their very nature create a group of people who are not full citizens, and who are easily exploited and abused. "It creates a permanent underclass of workers who are unable to fully participate in democracy," said AFL-CIO president John Sweeney. "The plan deepens the potential for abuse and exploitation of these workers, while undermining wages and labor protections for all workers."[3]

In contrast, Eliseo Medina, president of the SEIU (Service Employees International Union), whose father came to the United States under the bracero program, argues that this guest worker proposal avoids the problematic aspects of earlier programs. He declared the SEIU's support for the Senate bill. The Change to Win Coalition, which split from the AFL-CIO in 2005 and to which the SEIU now belongs, has not taken an official position on the matter. But some SEIU members disagreed so strongly with their union's position that they formed a new organization called "No Worker Is Illegal" to press the SEIU to revise its stance. "Guest-worker programs, further militarization of the border, and employer sanctions hurt all workers," they explain.[4]

Others point out that a temporary guest-worker program

is at odds with the jobs that migrant workers are filling. Only one in ten Mexican workers in the United States holds a temporary or seasonal job. "Rotating temporary workers through permanent jobs is simply not sound policy, and invites non-compliance with the terms of the programme by both migrants and employers," notes immigration specialist Wayne Cornelius.[5]

Meanwhile, states and local communities around the United States are discussing or implementing anti-immigrant regulations. Fifty-seven state-level bills were enacted in the first half of 2006. A few of these actually extended some rights to noncitizens, but the majority sought to further marginalize and exclude them. Especially popular were those restricting public benefits and those punishing unauthorized employment.[6]

Hazelton, Pennsylvania, Vista, California, and Milford, Massachusetts, are only three of dozens of cities that have passed local ordinances aimed against immigrants. The southern California town of Vista (population 72,000) now requires those who hire day laborers to "register with the city, display a certificate in their car windows and present written terms of employment to workers." Milford revised zoning laws to prevent unrelated adults from sharing housing. Hazelton's mayor signed the "Illegal Immigration Relief Act" to punish those who do business with, employ, or provide housing for undocumented immigrants.[7] In New Hampshire, local police in Hudson and New Ipswich have arrested undocumented immigrants for trespassing. (The courts struck down the charges.) The Arizona legislature passed a similar bill in April, 2006, though it was vetoed by the governor.[8]

While right-wing talk-show hosts have become notorious for their rather virulent anti-immigrant stances, polls show that in fact significant majorities of the population support the "comprehensive" approach that provides a route to legalization for undocumented immigrants currently in the country as well as increased border control. A Manhattan Institute survey of likely Republican voters found that 72 percent supported a plan along the lines of the Senate proposal.[9]

Much, however, depends on how the question is framed. A CNN poll commissioned by anti-immigrant commentator Lou Dobbs asked, "Do you approve or disapprove of the U.S. government deporting immigrants to the country they came from?" Sixty-seven percent answered, "approve." When asked whether they wanted to see the number of illegal immigrants increased, decreased, or stay the same, 67 percent said "decreased"—but only 34 percent followed up that they wanted to see all illegal immigrants deported.

Interestingly, the CNN/Dobbs poll found the most dramatic results when it asked, "When someone is arrested, do you think the police should be required to determine whether that person is a U.S. citizen?" and "When someone applies to a social service agency for assistance such as welfare or food stamps, do you think that agency should or should not be required to check whether that person is a citizen and record their citizenship status?" Eighty-three percent answered "yes" to the first, and 91 percent to the second.[10]

The AFL-CIO enthusiastically promotes Dobbs's *Exporting America: Why Corporate Greed Is Shipping American Jobs Overseas* on its "Union Shop" website.[11] Dobbs made common cause with the AFL-CIO on issues of outsourcing and free trade, making union representatives frequent guests on his show. He was lauded by AFL-CIO secretary-treasurer Richard Trumka, who called his show a "nightly crusade," and the *New York Teacher,* which called him "the working chump's champion."[12]

Dobbs parted with the unions, though, when the AFL-CIO began to move away from its anti-immigrant stance. Dobbs takes a populist line against immigration, arguing that "big business and labor groups are the beneficiaries of illegal immigration, the true costs are borne by taxpayers and working Americans."[13] "American working men and women are under the most vicious assault from so-called free trade, job outsourcing to cheap foreign labor markets, rising healthcare costs, a failing educational system, massive illegal immigration, and stagnant wages," Dobbs writes, taking unions to task for failing to protect their members'—and other working people's—interests.[14]

Still, despite the popularity of Dobbs and other virulently anti-immigrant media figures, public opinion overall seems to be decidedly less hysterical on the issue than are the voices that make it into the media. The Pew Hispanic Foundation found that 52 percent agreed that immigrants "are a burden because they take jobs, housing, and health-care," while 41 percent felt that immigrants "strengthen our country with their hard work and talents." These numbers varied fairly significantly by age, educational level, and economic level, with older people, people with only a high school education or less, and people who reported their personal finances as "only fair/poor" being more likely to feel immigrants were a burden. Interestingly, there was no significant difference between blacks and whites, although Hispanics were much more likely to see immigrants in positive terms.[15]

The Pew research brought out two additional, illuminating results. First, people who lived in areas with very few immigrants were much more likely to have negative views of immigrants than people who lived in areas with high concentrations of immigrants. In areas with low concentrations of immigrants, a full 67 percent felt that immigrants were a burden and only 27 percent felt that they strengthened the country, whereas in areas with many immigrants, 47 percent felt they were a burden and 48 percent felt they were a benefit.[16] This suggests that for many people, anti-immigrant sentiments come less from personal experience than from outside sources.

Second, the poll showed that despite the virulence of anti-immigrant rhetoric on talk shows and elsewhere, very few people, even those who said they were worried about immigrants taking jobs, housing, and health care, really considered the issue to be of major importance. Sixty-two percent said that the presence of immigrants in their communities had not significantly affected public services, and only 27 percent said that immigrants had negatively affected services.[17] When asked what the most important problem facing their local community was, 14 percent answered crime and violence, 14 percent said unemployment, and 12 percent said education. Between 5 and 10 percent each chose one of the following: crowding/traffic, roads, infrastructure, and government/politics. Only 4 percent saw immigration as the most important problem.[18]

Where, then, does the virulence of the debate come from? Why do politicians and commentators seem to think that immigration is such a divisive and hot-button issue, if the American public seems more concerned about traffic and road conditions, to say nothing of crime, unemployment, and education?

I'll suggest two possible explanations. One is that while large numbers of Americans don't share in the anti-immigrant fears and sentiments, those who do so feel very strongly and are very vocal. Their voices thus make a large and noisy impact in the public sphere.

The second is that elected officials, and commentators and talk-show hosts, are very much aware of the many Americans who are deeply disturbed by the growing economic inequalities, loss of quality of life, and deterioration of public services that have resulted from economic restructuring in the United States over the past thirty years. An ever-growing segment of the U.S. middle class lives "only a job loss, a medical problem, or an out-of-control credit card away from financial catastrophe."[19]

Not only do Americans feel that they are in an economically precarious situation, they also have little faith in their leaders to resolve the issues facing our society. One recent poll asked Americans to rate the level of trust they feel in the country's institutions. The levels of trust were appallingly low: only 3 percent trusted Congress, 7 percent trusted corporate leaders, 11 percent trusted the media, 24 percent trusted the president, and 29 percent trusted the courts.[20] Meanwhile, voter turnout rates in the United States hover between 50 percent and 60 percent—among the lowest in the industrialized world.[21]

Under such circumstances, it's not surprising that some members of Congress and the media resort to fearmongering and scapegoating as a way of trying to attract public attention and support. Immigrants present a convenient target. The level of noise, however, seems to be greater than anti-immigrant demagogues' actual ability to influence public opinion. Between 2000 and 2006, the numbers of Americans who believed that immigrants are a burden on the country did increase, from 38 percent to 52 percent, while those who believed they strengthened the country decreased from 50 percent to 41 percent. Still, between 1997 and 2006 the proportion believing that Latinos work very hard increased from 63 to 80 percent, the proportion believing that they often go on welfare decreased from 55 to 37 percent, and the proportion believing that they significantly increased crime rates decreased from 43 to 33 percent.[22]

Furthermore, the numbers who believe that immigrants take jobs from Americans has been on a fairly steady decline since 1983, when over 40 percent believed it. Today it's just

24 percent.[23] So it seems that the upsurge in anti-immigrant rhetoric and politicking may have inflamed small numbers of people, but that most people in the country, especially those who live in high-immigration areas, hold more measured views.

MYTH 16

THE OVERWHELMING VICTORY OF PROPOSITION 187 IN CALIFORNIA SHOWS THAT THE PUBLIC OPPOSES IMMIGRATION

When immigration-related issues have come up for a vote, as they did in 1994 with California's Proposition 187, the voting results don't always look like the poll results reported above. "Prop 187," billed as the "illegal alien initiative," passed with 59 percent of the vote—a significant majority.[1] The initiative would have prohibited undocumented immigrants from receiving public health and education services in the state, had not most of its provisions been quickly struck down by the courts as unconstitutional.

There are two reasons why the vote on Prop 187 does not seem to correspond to the more positive attitude about immigrants that the polls tend to show. One is that the campaign itself mobilized virulent anti-immigrant rhetoric—and fallacious arguments—that may have influenced public opinion. In addition, while polls use scientific methods to come up with a representative cross-section of the population, electoral voting merely records the opinions of those who choose to vote. In California's 1994 election, only 8.9 million people voted—fewer than half of those eligible.

"The demographic profile of voters in the 1994 election contrasts sharply with the state's larger adult population and its citizen adults who are eligible to vote," one analysis of the results concluded. "As a group, voters in 1994 are older, include more white non-Hispanics, are more conservative, have higher levels of income, are better educated, include fewer residents of Los Angeles County, and are more apt to be affiliated with Protestant religions."[2] By age, race, political affiliation, and religion, this election mobilized precisely those who were more likely to hold anti-immigrant views.

A couple of other facts stand out about the results. First, the poorest Californians—those earning under twenty thousand dollars a year—were more opposed to Prop 187 than any other income group. Not surprisingly, Latinos voted overwhelmingly against the initiative, and political liberals and Democrats also tended to oppose it. Interestingly, men supported Prop 187 much more than women did. Only 52 percent of blacks and Asians supported it, while 64 percent of whites did—and 69 percent of white men.[3]

Another study of the campaign tactics of the two sides notes that even the "No on 187" campaign failed to challenge the anti-immigrant message. Jan Adams, a leader of the anti-187 movement in northern California, explained that the professional political consultants who ran the campaign "concluded it was necessary to concede the problematic nature of immigration, but find something even more unpopular than 'illegal' immigrants to blame, preferably the Federal government for failing to police the border adequately. A second set of messages played on voters' fears: rampaging gangs of (brown) children pushed out of the schools; the spread of tuberculosis by untreated 'illegals'; and, the staple of anti-initiative campaigns, it would all lead to bureaucracy and cost too much."[4]

By failing to offer a counter to the anti-immigrant message promoted by the pro-187 campaign, the "no" campaign may have actually strengthened anti-immigrant sentiment and encouraged some people to vote "yes."

Although Prop 187 was struck down by the courts, many of its provisions were in fact implemented in 1996 through the Welfare Reform Act. The act carefully avoided the blatantly unconstitutional elements of Prop 187, like denying public education to undocumented immigrant children. But it effectively excluded immigrants, documented and undocumented, from almost all other public benefits.

Prop 187 also played an important role in President Clinton's decision to unleash an enormous new border control initiative. Anti-immigrant sentiment in the United States, according to Wayne Cornelius, is "broad but not very deep"—except when mobilized through campaigns like the 187 campaign. With the 1996 elections approaching and California a key to a Clinton victory, the president decided to capitalize on—and thus further fan the flames of—the anti-immigrant upsurge there. One former Clinton official recalled a deliberate decision to "put as much money into the INS as it could plausibly absorb."[5]

The approval of Prop 187 does not necessarily show the strength of anti-immigrant attitudes in the United States. It did, though, provide a lesson to politicians on the potential for inflaming, and benefiting from, these attitudes.

MYTH 17

IMMIGRATION IS A PROBLEM

Immigration is indeed a problem, but not in the way it's generally defined. Immigration is a humanitarian problem. People leave their homelands, their families, and their livelihoods and risk their lives. What is needed is a humanitarian solution: the creation of a new model of global economic integration—one that redistributes the planet's resources more equitably among its inhabitants, and one that respects and nourishes traditional peasant lifestyles.

Instead, U.S. policies have turned a humanitarian problem into a humanitarian disaster. U.S. foreign policies foster more, rather than less, global inequality. Domestic policies keep domestic inequality, and the demand for secondary-sector workers, high. And border enforcement policies have created a humanitarian crisis. The $20 billion that the United States has spent on militarizing the border in the past decade has had no appreciable effect on immigration levels, but it has caused thousands of deaths and untold human suffering.

One of the places where the problems created by U.S. immigration policies play out most dramatically is on the U.S.–Mexico border. Since 1994, the United States has poured money and resources into trying to close various stretches of the border. Rather than slowing unauthorized border crossings, the campaign has turned the border into a death zone. Between 1985 and mid-1992, some 175 immigrants were killed as they tried to navigate their way across the freeways in San Diego, the most common border crossing area. Between 1995, when "Operation Gatekeeper" went into effect, and the end of 2004, some three thousand died crossing the border, most in the deserts of Arizona, as the crossing points have been pushed farther and farther east.[1] Close to another 500 died in 2005.[2] And that's only documented deaths: the bones of others who were abandoned in the desert, dead or dying, remain to be found.

While the human cost of "Operation Gatekeeper" has been significant, it has had "no statistically significant effect" on the number of unauthorized crossings. Wayne Cornelius found that the only substantive change it has brought, as far as overall immigration trends are concerned, is that unauthorized migrants are likely to stay longer in the United States and to bring their families, because going home to visit has become so much more dangerous.[3]

Between 1993, when the new border enforcement program began, and 2000, the average length of an undocumented Mexican immigrant's stay rose from forty weeks to fifty weeks, then to seventy weeks by 2002. The composition of the Mexican undocumented population also shifted, away from the predominantly single male migrants of the past to approximately 50 percent women and children. Some 48,000 children cross the border each year, many of them coming to try to find a parent—especially a mother—who is already in the United States. One study of domestic workers in Los Angeles found that 82 percent of live-in nannies and 24 percent of housecleaners were women who had left children behind in their homelands.[4]

The greatest beneficiaries of the change were the smugglers. The cost of crossing illegally rose—from around $500 in 1993 to $2,500 in 2004.[5] Border smuggling grew from a small-scale, individual operation to encompass sophisticated rings with links to organized crime and drug trafficking.[6] A Mexican study found over one hundred large-scale smuggling rings operating in 2004.[7]

The real victims are people like María Eugenia Martínez, a thirty-nine-year-old mother of eight from the indigenous region of Huehuetenango, Guatemala. Huehuetenango was one of the regions hardest hit by the counterinsurgency of the 1980s in Guatemala. While genocide against the country's indigenous population has five-hundred-year-old roots, the war of the 1980s was also a manifestation of U.S. post–World War II policies. In 1954 the United States orchestrated the overthrow of Guatemala's elected government, deeming it too soft on Communism. It put into place a series of ferociously right-wing military regimes, which ruled by terror until the mid-1990s.

Martínez's hometown of El Terrero was one of the areas the army considered to be a guerrilla stronghold, which meant that the entire population was treated as the enemy. Eighty percent of Huehuetenango province's inhabitants, primarily indigenous Mam, Chuj, and Kanjobal Maya people, fled their homes under army attack between 1980 and 1981. Some ended up in refugee camps just across the border in Chiapas, Mexico.[8] Others made it to the United States, especially Los Angeles. By 1990, Los Angeles had 159,000 Guatemalans recorded in the census—as usual, the actual population was probably much higher. Many of them were women domestic workers.[9]

Martínez, however, came in 2003, well after the signing of the peace accords in 1996. During the first years after the accords thousands of refugees returned from Mexico. But the economic devastation of the war had led to a continued high level of out-migration, overwhelmingly to the United States and often following links that had already been established.

Martínez had a half-brother and cousins in a Central American neighborhood in downtown Los Angeles. The situation in her hometown was becoming intolerable: her husband was abusive, and the money that she earned selling homemade sausages in a market stall wasn't enough to send her younger children to high school. So she did what so many others were doing: she crossed the border illegally, and joined her relatives in Los Angeles. She was working at a garment factory there when she was picked up and deported a little over a year later, in June 2004.[10]

About a million Guatemalans were living in the United States in 2005. Ten percent of them came from Huehuetenango, and over 35 percent lived in Los Angeles.[11] Martínez's experience was part of a much larger story.[12]

Her job in Los Angeles allowed her to send home money

for her children's education and for her older son's wedding. Again, she was not alone: over one-third of Guatemala's population received some of the $3 billion in remittances that migrants to the United States sent home in 2005.[13] Deported across the border and deposited in Tijuana, Martínez wanted to get back to Los Angeles, to her job, as quickly as possible.

Crossing the border in Tijuana was extremely difficult, so Martínez and several others traveled 150 miles east toward Mexicali. It's easier to cross the unguarded border in the desert between Tijuana and Mexicali, but it means an eight- to ten-hour hike through remote trails in punishing heat.

Martínez's group succeeded in getting across the border. But after four hours of hiking in hundred-degree heat with little water, she began to suffer from heat exhaustion and finally collapsed at the side of the trail. Part of the group continued, but when their water ran out they panicked and turned back to Mexico along a different trail. Martínez's sun-blackened, decomposing body was discovered by a Border Patrol helicopter days later.[14] Her story reveals the real "problem" of immigration—a problem that few U.S. citizens ever see.

MYTH 18

COUNTRIES NEED TO CONTROL WHO GOES IN AND OUT

Governments have often tried to control the size and makeup of their populations by how they establish their borders, by expelling or exterminating groups of people within their national borders, by controlling movement and settlement, and by controlling reproduction inside their frontiers. Generally, when we study how governments have done this in the past, we are horrified.

There's a parallel between racial thinking and economic thinking here. One pattern is that colonizers fear losing their racial control over those they colonize. There is talk of race suicide, and worries that people of color are reproducing far too quickly and will overwhelm the white population. Population control becomes a method for preserving white dominance.

The economic pattern is that in societies divided between haves and have-nots, the haves often see eliminating the have-nots as the best solution to inequality, rather than redistributing the resources. As a solution to poverty, the haves propose methods to make poor people stop reproducing.

Because the division of the world, and of individual societies, into haves and have-nots has been so structured by conquest and ideas of racial superiority, the racial and the economic arguments are often two sides of the same coin. And the solution too is the same: find ways to eradicate, and justify the eradication of, poor people of color.

Let's look at some examples. In the United States, Native Americans were the original aliens who had to be expelled from the land in order to create a white, English society here. English migrants had no intention of assimilating into the land they migrated to: they wanted to replace the societies that existed there. "The tribes which occupied the countries now constituting the Eastern States were annihilated or have melted away to make room for the whites," President Andrew Jackson explained in an address to Congress in 1830. This history justified his own Indian removal program, "the benevolent policy of the Government, steadily pursued for nearly thirty years, in relation to the removal of the Indians beyond the white settlements," which he announced was "approaching to a happy consummation."[1]

African Americans constituted a different kind of alien in white America's midst: not potential citizens, yet necessary as a labor force. So they were forced to be physically present, while legally, they were nonpersons. Until the 1870s, that is. After the brief experiment with Reconstruction, white society embarked on a century of African American expulsion. Jim Crow laws, lynchings, and regulations drove African Americans out of institutions, towns, counties, and even states.

Like African Americans, the Chinese were used for labor, denied citizenship, then excluded. For Mexicans, temporary worker programs and periodic waves of deportation followed the same pattern. The incarceration of Japanese, and people of Japanese descent, during World War II reiterated the message: this is a white country, and you are not wanted among us.

Advances in technology, combined with the development of the pseudoscience of eugenics, provided another means of population control. When they weren't physically driven out or slaughtered, people of color were the subject of eugenics campaigns to try to curtail their reproduction. The same "eugenical thinking" that was behind immigration restrictions was also behind anti-miscegenation laws aimed at keeping the races separate, and anti-reproduction strategies aimed at preventing population growth among those considered racially inferior.

Part of the rationale for eugenics policies was that medical and social advances had interfered with the process of natural selection, which would have naturally eliminated the inferior races in the absence of human intervention. As geographer James A. Tyner explains, "especially pronounced was a popular belief that welfare and charity programs were counteracting the 'bloody hand' of evolution. Rather than succumbing to nature's law of 'survival of the fittest,' misguided philanthropy—including minimum wages, set working hours, free public education, public health reforms—was enabling inferior peoples to live longer and to reproduce."[2]

Madison Grant, the U.S. scientific racist thinker, wrote in 1918 that "the most practical and hopeful method of race improvement is through the elimination of the least desirable elements of the nation by depriving them of the power to contribute to future generations."[3] His ideas were behind the 1920s immigration restrictions and also provided scholarly justification for sterilization campaigns directed against citizens who were considered undesirable. From Vermont to California to the Deep South to Puerto Rico, nonwhite women were sterilized in disproportionate numbers by zealous doctors intent on improving the race.[4]

California, consistently the state with the highest rates of involuntary sterilization, kept its law on the books from 1909 to 1979. By 1942, over 15,000 people had been sterilized. Mexican Americans were sterilized at a rate double their proportion of the population, and African Americans at four times their proportion.[5]

Shortly after taking Puerto Rico in 1898, U.S. officials started to worry about "overpopulation" on the island. "It was first used in policy debates to explain off-island labor contracts, where agents from U.S. business or agriculture would offer transportation to places like Hawaii, Arizona, or Georgia, in exchange for work contracts . . . By the 1930s, however, the term 'overpopulation' had acquired another meaning, one that blamed excessive sexuality and fertility for the poverty of the island as a whole."[6]

Women's studies professor Laura Briggs explains that

"by 1932, responding to the problem of 'overpopulation' had become the cornerstone of federal policy in Puerto Rico."[7] Promoters of birth control policies in Puerto Rico believed that "it was better to prevent poor or dark-skinned people from being born."[8] In the 1940s and '50s, U.S. pharmaceutical companies used the island as a giant laboratory for contraceptive research, including early trials of the birth control pill.[9]

High rates of sterilization of blacks and Native Americans also continued into the second half of the century. In the 1950s, sterilization, "preponderantly aimed at African American and poor women, began to be wielded by state courts and legislatures as a punishment for bearing illegitimate children or as extortion to ensure ongoing receipt of family assistance."[10] Sterilization rates rose again, especially after the War on Poverty in the 1960s introduced federally funded sterilizations through Medicaid and the Office of Economic Opportunity, leading to what one analyst called "widespread sterilization abuse" during the 1960s and '70s. Between 1960 and 1974 over 100,000 sterilizations were carried out annually.[11]

The Indian Health Service began providing family planning services in 1965. Protests and federal investigations revealed that regulations requiring consent were routinely violated. In an article in *American Indian Quarterly*, Ph.D. student Jane Lawrence cited a study by the Health Research Group in Washington, D.C., that found that "the majority of physicians were white, Euro-American males who believed that they were helping society by limiting the number of births in low-income, minority families. They assumed that they were enabling the government to cut funding for Medicaid and welfare programs while lessening their own personal tax burden to support the programs."[12] Between 25 percent and 50 percent of Native American women were sterilized in the 1970s. A study by a Native American physician concluded that Indian women often agreed to sterilization because they were told that otherwise they would lose their children or their welfare benefits.[13]

In spite of a national outcry when Dr. Helen Rodríguez-Trías discovered rates of sterilization approaching 40 percent in Puerto Rico in 1965—prompting federal legislation to restrict involuntary or coerced sterilizations—federally funded sterilization programs continued to target women of color. Over 40 percent of Puerto Rican women were still getting sterilized in the 1980s.[14] Studies in the 1970s and 1990s showed that black women had double the sterilization rate of white women.[15] Former Reagan administration official William J. Bennett revealed that "eugenical thinking" has not completely disappeared from our culture with his notorious comment that "you could abort every black baby in this country, and your crime rate would go down."[16]

Of course the United States is not the only country to have used exclusionary citizenship, expulsions, racial purification campaigns, sterilizations, and eugenics to try to create an ethnically homogenous nation. Jews, the quintessential "others" in the European nation-states in which they lived, were subject to periodic expulsions and exterminations there. They then reversed the balance in Palestine, where they drove out Palestinian inhabitants and created laws allowing Jews who had never set foot there to "return," while Palestinians became aliens forbidden to return to their homes in 1948 and again in 1967.

Immigration restrictions against people of color in the United States have historically responded to the same logic as other forms of population control. Today's immigration restrictions do not explicitly mention race, but they still apply, overwhelmingly, to people of color. And they still respond to the idea that governments should mandate the composition of the populations within their territories, and ensure that socially dominant groups remain numerically dominant.

An interesting twist on this logic in the United States has been the move to take children away from sectors of the population being eliminated and have them raised by the dominant sectors. The Native American boarding school program starting in the late 1800s was one early example of a dominant society trying to culturally and racially remake the population by removing children from their families.

Governments ranging from Franco's Spain in the 1940s to the dictatorships of Argentina in the 1970s and El Salvador in the 1980s engaged in programs of abducting children of supposed leftists and placing them for adoption.[17] In the words of women's studies professor Laura Briggs,

> Raising the "orphans" of colonized people is a very familiar practice. From the nineteenth century French orphanages in Indochina to U.S. children's homes in

> Puerto Rico in the early years of the twentieth, managing children and raising youth to belong to a different culture from that of their ancestors has a history. Indeed the white settler colonies of the British empire—the United States, Canada, Australia—made acculturating native children in boarding schools as indispensable a part of their policies toward indigenous people as war and reservations.[18]

The American Association of Indian Affairs (AAIA) noted in the 1960s that an astonishing one in four Native American children in some states had been removed from parental care into adoptive, foster, or institutional homes. In the '60s and '70s, Native American and African American groups including the AAIA and the National Association of Black Social Workers protested the ongoing state-mandated removal of children from these communities and their placement with white families.[19]

The current growth in international adoptions illuminates the continuing ironies in U.S. immigration policies. Most international adoptions are carried out by white, middle-class families from countries whose inhabitants face severe restrictions in trying to come to the United States. For the children entering white families, however, law and practice smooth the way. In the summer of 2006, as Israeli bombs systematically flattened the country of Lebanon, Lebanese desperate to escape to safety found the doors of the so-called liberal democracies slammed in their faces. Calling to mind what Paul Farmer had said about Haiti in the early 1990s, the country was coming to resemble a burning building with no exits. In the midst of it all, the *Boston Globe* reported cheerily that "Logan Edward Maroon Gabriel is home, finally." A Salem, New Hampshire, woman was waiting in Beirut to complete the adoption of the baby when the invasion unfolded. In contrast to the hundreds of thousands of Lebanese who had no way out, this baby's papers were quickly put in order, and the beaming family pictured prominently in the newspaper as they were welcomed by "100 cheering relatives and friends."[20]

MYTH 19

WE NEED TO PROTECT OUR BORDERS TO PREVENT CRIMINALS AND TERRORISTS FROM ENTERING THE COUNTRY

The potential that a citizen will commit a crime or even a terrorist act is just as real as the potential that an immigrant will. No country has a monopoly on violent lawbreakers, and in no country are they nonexistent. The rule of law, and the lawful prosecution of those who commit crimes, makes a lot more sense than closing borders as a way to reduce criminality.

Terrorist acts in the United States have been committed by citizens and by immigrants, and for causes related to domestic as well as international issues. In 2000, the FBI reported no incidents of international terrorism carried out inside the United States and eight incidents of domestic terrorism, all carried out by U.S. citizens belonging to animal rights groups or environmental groups. In 2001, there were twelve incidents of domestic terrorism, one (the September 11 attacks) of international terrorism, and one (the anthrax-laced-letter incidents) of unknown origins. Environmental and animal rights groups (in this case the Earth Liberation

Front and the Animal Liberation Front) were again the apparent perpetrators of several of the twelve domestic incidents, joined in 2001 by two carried out by anti-abortion activists.[1]

Those involved in the 9/11 attacks, which in scale dwarfed the other attacks taking place in the United States, were not citizens. However, all but four were legally in the country at the time of the attacks, having entered on tourist or student visas. A study of forty-eight "militant Islamic terrorists" who committed crimes in the United States, by the anti-immigration Center for Immigration Studies, found that thirty-six of them were in the country legally at the time they committed crimes, and seventeen were either permanent residents or naturalized citizens. Those who were not permanent residents had received visas—mostly tourist visas—to come to the country, and most of them had not violated the terms of their visas.[2] Not even the highest fence or the most militarized border in the world would have kept them out. Their crimes were crimes of violence, not crimes of immigration.

It's true that there have been in the past, and may be in the future, individuals working with international terrorist organizations who want to enter the United States. However, these are actually among the *least* likely people to risk arrest and death trying to cross the border illegally. It's much more likely that members of an international organization like Al-Qaeda will, like the September 11 perpetrators, use perfectly legal channels to get into the United States.

Does this mean that we need to do better, or different,

screening of those who want to enter the United States by legal means? Possibly. But the idea that screening people who cross borders is an effective way to deter terrorist attacks is also a kind of a mirage. Just as U.S. planes cross international borders to drop bombs, usually without going through any kind of immigration control process, so could the United States become the victim of international attack, regardless of its border control policies. The planes that flew into the twin towers on September 11 happened to take off in Boston . . . But they could just as well have taken off from some other country. Hijackers, like invaders, have proven quite able to cross borders and kill people without permission. And criminals can be born anywhere, including inside the United States. There is just no logical relationship between border security and the prevention of terrorism.

Is there, then, nothing that can be done to prevent future terrorist attacks? First, those of us who live in the United States should remember that the number of civilians killed by U.S. military attacks on other countries has far, far exceeded the number of U.S. civilians killed by attacks on the United States, or against U.S. citizens elsewhere. So curbing U.S. military aggression would probably be the most effective way to achieve a global reduction in attacks on unarmed civilians.

As far as preventing future attacks against U.S. targets, a combination of two approaches seems most likely to achieve that result. On one hand, seeking to reduce global tensions, and in particular U.S. unilateralism and aggression, could substantially reduce anti-Americanism in other countries.

Second, effective police and investigative work—abiding by international law, international agreements, and the Geneva Conventions—at least offers the possibility of working toward a world ruled by law, in which criminals are prosecuted under the rule of law for the crimes they commit, and those not accused of any crime are spared the fate of becoming collateral damage.

MYTH 20

IF PEOPLE BREAK OUR LAWS BY IMMIGRATING ILLEGALLY, THEY ARE CRIMINALS AND SHOULD BE DEPORTED

As we've seen, the history of our country has included many laws that today look unjust and discriminatory. The original laws of this country upheld slavery and limited citizenship to white men. Later laws justified lynching and segregation. When we look back at history, we generally honor the people who broke those laws. Rosa Parks broke the law when she refused to move to the back of the bus. Harriet Tubman broke the law when she fled slavery and helped to create the Underground Railroad.

Immigration laws are very different from the laws that we usually have in mind when we talk about people breaking the law. "Breaking the law" conjures up images of assaults, thefts, murders—violations of laws that were created to protect people from harm.

Like other discriminatory legislation in our country's history, immigration laws define and differentiate legal status on the basis of arbitrary attributes. Immigration laws create unequal rights. People who break immigration laws don't cause harm or even potential harm (unlike, for example, drunk driving, which creates the potential for harm even if no accident occurs). Rather, people who break immigration laws do things that are perfectly legal for others, but denied to them—like cross a border or, even more commonly, simply exist.

Some undocumented immigrants crossed the border "illegally," but many in fact obtained legal permission to cross the border and entered the country on visas that allowed them to stay temporarily. When the visa expired, they became "illegal" overnight.

Some citizens wonder why immigrants don't simply "follow the rules" and do the appropriate paperwork, or renew their visas, or become citizens, thus becoming "legal." The reason they don't is the same as the reason that Rosa Parks didn't sit "legally" in the front of the bus, or Harriet Tubman didn't "legally" emancipate herself from slavery: because the law was designed *not* to allow certain groups of people to have the rights that others enjoy.

"If I had the resources and the connections to apply to come legally," one undocumented Mexican immigrant explained, "I wouldn't need to leave Mexico to work in this country." Or, in the words of Pew Hispanic Center demographer Jeffrey Passel, "For most Mexicans, there is no line to get in."[1]

For would-be immigrants from the Philippines, for example, the U.S. government was, as of mid-2006, granting visas to people who applied as long ago as 1984. The way the preference system works, if a Filipino has no immediate family in the United States, he or she basically can't even get in line to wait for a visa. For people in the "fourth preference" category—brothers and sisters of U.S. citizens—visas were just being made available for those who applied in 1984. If you fell into the "first preference"—unmarried children of U.S. citizens, including minor children—Immigration Services was, in 2006, allocating visas to those who applied in 1992.[2]

What happened to an eighty-one-year-old Haitian Baptist pastor, Joseph Dantica, can help to illustrate the strange netherworld dividing "legal" from "illegal" immigrants. Dantica held a valid multiple-entry visa to the United States. In October 2004, armed Haitian gangs attacked his home and his church in a poor neighborhood of Port-au-Prince, threatening to kill him if he did not give them money they demanded. After going into hiding for several days, Dantica used his visa to get on a flight to the United States, where several of his family members lived.

When he went through immigration in Miami, his visa was approved and stamped for entry. Then the immigration official asked him how long he intended to stay in the United States. When he said that he was planning to ask for political asylum, fearing that he'd be killed if he returned to Haiti, he was arrested.

The law permitted his entrance into the United States on a tourist visa. The law also permitted him to ask for asylum in the United States. But the law also said that he would be arrested for doing these things. Haitians who request asylum from inside the United States are considered guilty until proven innocent.

In Dantica's case, immigration officials confiscated his medications when they jailed him, and after four days he died in the Krome Detention Center. Family members in the United States were denied the right to see him as he lay dying.[3]

Technically, the law authorized Dantica's arrest. If he had been Cuban, instead of Haitian, he would not have been arrested. Under the 1995 "wet foot, dry foot" policy, Cubans are automatically eligible for asylum if they set foot on U.S. territory. That's why author Tom Miller, commenting on the immigrants' rights demonstrations in 2006, suggested that "what they really want is to be treated like Cubans . . . [Cubans] don't need to wade the Rio Grande or walk the Sonoran Desert—they can simply stroll up to any port of entry along the two-thousand-mile border and say to the U.S. immigration inspector, 'Soy cubana. ¿me permite entrar?' I'm Cuban, mind if I come in? And the answer is almost always, 'come on in!' "[4]

Dantica is only one out of tens of thousands of immigrants each year who commit a victimless crime that is illegal because of who they are, not because of what they did. Mexicans cross the border "illegally" because they are not allowed to cross the border legally. The law discriminates by making it illegal for some people to do what is perfectly legal for others.

MYTH 21

THE PROBLEMS THIS BOOK RAISES ARE SO HUGE THAT THERE'S NOTHING WE CAN DO ABOUT THEM

In this book I've tried to show that immigration is part of an interconnected global system that has been shaped by history and economics. People have been moving around the earth ever since they stood upright millions of years ago. National borders, and attempts to govern the flows of migration from above, are only a few hundred years old.

Today's immigration is structured by contemporary relationships among countries and regions, and by their history of economic inequality. Unequal economic relationships should be changed—not because they lead to migration, but because they lead to human suffering and an unsustainable world. High levels of migration are a symptom of a global economic system that privileges the few at the expense of the many. It could be called capitalism, it could be called neoliberalism, it could be called globalization, it could be called neocolonialism. As long as it keeps resources unequally distributed in the world, you're going to have people escaping the regions that are deliberately kept poor and violent and seeking freedom in the places where the world's resources have been concentrated: in the countries that have controlled, and been the beneficiaries of, the global economic system that took shape after 1492.

If our goal is to slow migration, then the best way to do so is to work for a more equitable global system. But slowing migration is an odd goal, if the real problem is global inequality. Fences and borders might be touted as a curb on migration, but in fact they serve to harden global inequality.

Of course global inequality can't be transformed overnight. And immigration policy is only one piece of a much larger system. It may seem overwhelming to try to imagine how to get from our current state to a more just and egalitarian world.

Still, there are certainly concrete steps that we could take to make our immigration policy more humane. A more humane immigration policy would reduce human suffering by a significant, if limited, amount. It would not, in and of itself, make much difference in the way the world is structured. If changes in immigration policy were accompanied by similar small steps to ameliorate glaring injustices in other areas, though, we might actually be on our way to creating a better world.

In a more equal world, border issues would cease to hold the importance that they do. Consider the example of the European Union. Given the relatively equal distribution of resources, power, and opportunity among the countries of Europe, the virtual elimination of borders among them was not an earth-shattering event. Another example of relatively open borders is that which exists among the various states in the United States. Residents of Massachusetts can travel freely to Connecticut, through an entirely unpoliced border. Still, while there they must obey Connecticut's speed limit, tax, and seat belt laws. It's entirely possible for open borders to coexist with orderly administration and a state of law.

Our current immigration policy is so overloaded with inhuman, and inhumane, provisions that improving it would be first and foremost an exercise in eliminating its most baleful characteristics. We could start by rolling back the punitive and discriminatory changes that have been made in the last several decades, especially in the 1996 Illegal Immigration Reform and Immigrant Responsibility Act.[1] Revoking some of the most draconian elements of that law would be a logical first step in a process aimed at eventually guaranteeing full equality before the law for immigrants.

Another step forward would be to reverse the militarization of the border that began with Operation Gatekeeper in 1993. The decriminalization of border crossing would encourage almost all would-be immigrants to pass through established inspection stations, just as, for example, the vast majority of U.S. citizens do when they travel to Mexico or Canada. Would-be immigrants would no longer have to turn to smugglers and risky desert crossings. Those in the United States could return home freely. Families could be reunited.

Extending full legal rights to all immigrants would go far toward eliminating the economic exploitation of immigrant workers. Some immigrants—just as some citizens do—would probably still work under the table. But employers would no longer be able to use the threat of deportation, and workers would no longer be subject to the constant fear of discovery. Their ability to stand up for their rights, and to unionize, would be greatly enhanced. These first steps would put us on the road to a humane immigration policy.

Would these steps lead to a huge influx in immigration? It's hard to tell, but most of the signs suggest that they would not. The increasingly punitive, dangerous, and exploitative policies of the past two decades have not led to any decrease in immigration—just the opposite. Immigration has steadily increased as anti-immigrant policies have become harsher. As I've tried to show in this book, the main causes of immigration are structural, economic, and historical, and they have to do with global relationships and global inequality.

Taking steps to humanize immigration policy would not, of course, eliminate the global and domestic economic inequalities that are the underlying cause of migration. But there are also small steps we could conceive of taking toward creating a more equal society, and a more equal world. While these steps would inevitably lead to a slowing of migration, that's not the main reason we should follow them. We should work for a more just world for moral, ethical, and humanitarian reasons. Migration would be reduced because poor people's lives and livelihoods would become more sustainable—which is a worthy end on its own.

Domestically, we could think about reweaving and strengthening the social safety net that has been so frayed since the 1970s. Working for national health care and universal preschool might be a place to start. Or restructuring the tax system so that corporations and the super-rich pay their fair share. Or enforcing corporate accountability toward workers and communities. We could work toward a thirty-hour work week and full employment.

Globally, we could forgive Third World debt and create a system of democratic oversight for U.S. corporations operating abroad. We could respect the sovereignty of governments like Cuba's, Venezuela's, and Bolivia's, which are experimenting with different economic models. We could eliminate military "aid" that is used primarily, in Latin America, to repress domestic movements for social change.

Trying to build a new world of more just relationships is a worthy goal in and of itself, regardless of the effect it might have on migration. But a more just world will, inevitably, also lead to a drop in migration. Some migrants leave their homelands for fun, adventure, or curiosity. The vast majority, though, leave because they have no alternative. They leave their homes, their families, and their loved ones as a last resort.

More of the same kinds of foreign policies that have brought the world to its present state will not change the structures of global inequality. More invasions, more foreign domination, more free trade, and more foreign investment are not the answer. A different kind of global system would necessarily entail a more just distribution of the world's resources. It would mean that the industrialized countries—led by the United States, by far the world's largest consumer of resources—would have to lower their levels of consumption, so that there would be something left for the rest of the world.

Uruguayan journalist Eduardo Galeano wrote in 1992:

> The average American consumes as much as 50 Haitians . . . What would happen if the fifty Haitians consumed as many cars, as many televisions, as many refrigerators or as many luxury goods as the one American? Nothing. Nothing would ever happen again. We would have to change planets. Ours, which is already close to catastrophe, couldn't take it.
>
> The precarious equilibrium of the world depends on the perpetuation of injustice. So that some can consume more, people must continue to consume less. To keep people in their place, the system produces armaments. Incapable of fighting poverty, the system fights the poor.[2]

Fifteen years after Galeano wrote these words, today's war on immigrants continues the fight against the poor.

EPILOGUE

As I was finishing my work on this book, I had the opportunity to travel to a remote region of Colombia and see firsthand, from the other side, some of the global economic changes that have contributed to the surge in immigration in recent decades—and will continue to do so in the future.

Colombia's Guajira peninsula is one of the poorest and most isolated regions of the country. Except for a few tourist spots along the coast, few outsiders or even Colombians travel there. Because it borders Venezuela and abuts the Caribbean Sea, it has maintained a small-scale local economy of trade and smuggling for centuries—everything from precious metals to cigarettes, to illegal drugs, to gasoline.

The population in the region is made up of indigenous Wayuu people—the largest indigenous group in Colombia—and small Afro-Colombian and mestizo communities. The Wayuu trace their presence in the peninsula to before the Spanish conquest. The Afro-Colombian communities' oral histories recount that they descend from enslaved Africans who rebelled and freed themselves on a ship bound for the Caribbean. They took over the ship and landed on the Guajira, making their way inland, and founded the original four communities there.

Public services are scarce to nonexistent. In the northern desert region, the mostly Wayuu inhabitants are seminomadic herders. Organized in matrilineal clans, they travel with their herds to where there is water. Many of the women are monolingual in the Wayuu language, though many men also speak Spanish. In the southern part of the peninsula, both Afro-Colombian and indigenous communities found fertile farmlands and depended on the Ranchería River that runs down the peninsula as a source of water.

Economic development came crashing into the Guajira in the early 1980s in the form of what soon became the world's largest open-pit coal mine. The U.S.-based Exxon Corporation entered into a joint venture with the Colombian government to explore and exploit the mine, which was later privatized and sold to a consortium of some of the world's largest mining multinationals: BHP Billiton, Glencore, and Anglo-American.

The mine undeniably brought economic development to the region. But it was exactly the kind of distorted development that destroys traditional farming communities and sets the stage for migration.

The mine gobbled up formerly productive lands and turned them into a giant hole in the ground, thirty-five miles long and five miles wide. It churned up a dust that blankets and smothers the region for miles around the mine itself. It fouled the Ranchería River, leaving the small communities with no water source.

"We have no source of work to support our families," wrote members of the indigenous community of Tamaquito in the summer of 2006. "We don't even have any income with which to buy our women the materials they need for their weavings . . . We are getting sick because of the contamination of the Cerrejón mine, and we have no land left to cultivate. We also cannot raise animals because they die. When we do plant something, we cannot harvest it because the coal dust kills it."

After being subject to the same kinds of conditions for years, the Afro-Colombian community of Tabaco was razed in the summer of 2001 as the mine continued its inexorable expansion. "I want to say a little about how we lived in Tabaco," a former resident told our visiting delegation five years later. "Life was rich, we shared, no one suffered because we shared what we had. There was a river near the town. We had land. We walked freely all over the territory. The last nine years we have had no land to work, we are displaced, we have no lodging. I had a farm, I had animals, but they ran me off, so I lost everything . . . I raised my twelve children there. When we lost my land I wasn't able to continue educating my children. I still own a small piece of land but it is in the middle of the company's land and we can't even get to it."

For the past five hundred years the global trend, accelerating in the past fifty years or so, has been one of rural–urban migration. Peasant farmers have historically been tenaciously attached to their land. The voices of the people of Tamaquito and Tabaco echo the voices of millions of people displaced from their small farms over the centuries.

Enormous amounts of violence and coercion, and human suffering, were necessary to separate Africans from their lands and bring them to the Americas as forced laborers, to separate indigenous communities in the Americas from their lands to make the lands available for plantations and mines.

Once the millennial connection that ties peasants to their lands is broken, it is almost impossible to restore. Once their children leave the land to go to the cities, almost nothing could convince them to return to a life of farming.

It's a painful, heartbreaking, and almost irreversible process. It's already happened in much of the world: 48 percent of the world's population lived in urban areas in 2003, and the proportion is expected to exceed 50 percent in 2007, for the first time in human history.[1]

Visiting the Guajira gave me an unmatchable firsthand view of the process, just at the moment of dispossession. The small farming communities in the area around the mine were barely hanging on. Their farmlands had been taken over by the mine, their water source contaminated, the air was thick with dust, their animals were dying and their children were coughing constantly. But the people were adamant. "I'm a farmer. That's all I know how to do. We want land." This was their unending refrain.

"Why don't they just leave?" asked a U.S. embassy representative when we met with him after our visit to the Guajira and described the unbearable situation of the villagers there. Why, indeed? Where would they go? To join the two to three million other displaced people in Colombia in the shantytowns surrounding the major urban areas? To forage in the garbage dumps? To the United States?

What seemed so dramatic was catching these communities in a historical moment in which they still were utterly committed to maintaining their communal, agricultural lives: lives that were being undermined and destroyed by modernization.

If one goal of a humane migration policy is to reduce human suffering, then the needs and desires of peasant communities around the world that are struggling to maintain their traditional lifestyles and cultures should be central. Migration may not be clearly good or bad in and of itself, but the destruction of communities and cultures around the world is indisputably harmful to the people who live in them.

TIMELINE

1790 First naturalization law passed, restricting naturalization to "free white persons."[1]

1798 Alien and Sedition Acts provide for deportation of "dangerous" aliens.

1803 Louisiana Purchase doubles the size of U.S. territory, incorporating new populations.

1808 Importation of slaves prohibited.

1819 First federal immigration legislation requires reporting of all entries.

1830 Indian Removal Act leads to deportation of 100,000 Native Americans to west of the Mississippi.

1848 Treaty of Guadalupe Hidalgo expands the borders of the United States to the Pacific. Mexican residents given the option of declaring U.S. or Mexican citizenship.

1855 Immigrant women granted citizenship automatically upon marriage to a citizen, or upon an immigrant husband's naturalization.

1857 Dred Scott decision mandates that African Americans cannot be citizens.

1864 Contract Labor Law permits recruitment of foreign workers.

1868 Fourteenth Amendment grants citizenship to African Americans born in the U.S.

1870 Naturalization Act allows "white persons and persons of African descent" to naturalize.

1875 Convicts and prostitutes prohibited from entering country.

1882 Chinese Exclusion Act prohibits entry of Chinese for ten years.

Head tax of fifty cents imposed on immigrants.

Long-distance and seasonal Mexican migration grows with Chinese exclusion.

1885 Contract Labor Law prohibits entry by sea of workers recruited abroad (i.e., continues to allow recruitment of Mexican contract workers).

1891 Bureau of Immigration established under the Treasury Department to oversee and enforce federal immigration law.

Steamship companies required to return immigrants who fall into excluded categories to their place of origin.

1892 Ellis Island opened to screen incoming immigrants arriving from Europe.

1898 United States takes Puerto Rico, Guam, Philippines, and Hawaii as "territories." Residents are not granted citizenship, but as "nationals" they can enter the continental U.S.

1902 Chinese Exclusion Act renewed indefinitely.

1903 Anarchists, epileptics, polygamists, and beggars ruled inadmissible.

Bureau of Immigration transferred to the Department of Commerce and Labor.

1906 Knowledge of English required for naturalization.

Bureau of Immigration becomes Bureau of Immigration and Naturalization (the two are split in 1913 and reunited in 1933 under the Department of Labor as the Immigration and Naturalization Service).

First implementation of inspections at the Mexican border, primarily aimed at excluding Chinese entering through Mexico.

1907 Gentleman's Agreement with Japan restricts Japanese immigration.

Head tax is raised.

People with physical or mental defects, tuberculosis, and children unaccompanied by a parent are excluded.

Women lose citizenship upon marrying a noncitizen.

1917 Asiatic barred zone prohibits all immigration from Asia.

Literacy requirement established for immigrants from Europe.

Temporary guest-worker program exempts Mexicans from literacy requirement and head tax.

Puerto Ricans granted citizenship.

1918 Passport Act requires official documentation for

entry into the United States. Border Crossing Cards issued for Canadians and Mexicans.

1921 Quota Act limits European immigrants to 3 percent of each European nationality present in the U.S. in 1910. Visa issued in home country now required for entry. Non-Europeans are not included in the act: Asians are still barred, immigrants from the Western Hemisphere are allowed unlimited entry, and Africans are ignored.

1922 Mexican guest-worker program abolished.

Women's citizenship separated from that of their husbands (except if a woman marries an alien who is racially ineligible for citizenship, in which case she loses her citizenship).

1924 Quota Act revised to 2 percent of each nationality based on numbers in U.S in 1890. Still applies only to Europeans.

Border Patrol created.

Native Americans born in the United States granted citizenship (but still not allowed to naturalize).

1929 1924 Quota Act made permanent.

1930 Deportation of millions of Mexicans begins.

1934 Philippine Independence Act turns the Philippines into a commonwealth; Filipinos are no longer "nationals"; Philippines granted an immigration quota of 50.

1940 Alien Registration Act/Smith Act. Provides penalties, including deportation of noncitizens, for subversive activities. Requires fingerprinting and registration of all aliens.

"Descendants of races indigenous to the Western Hemisphere" allowed to naturalize.

1941 Internment of "enemy aliens" (primarily Japanese) begins. 120,000 Japanese Americans incarcerated by 1945.

1942 Bracero Program established for contracting of temporary agricultural workers from Mexico.

1943 Chinese Exclusion Law repealed, and Chinese allowed to become naturalized citizens. China granted a quota of 105.

British West Indies program established for importation of temporary agricultural workers from the BWI to eleven eastern states (especially Florida).

1945 War Brides Act allows immigration of foreign women married to members of the U.S. armed forces.

1946 Filipinos and (Asian) Indians allowed to naturalize (other Asians, including Koreans, Japanese, and Southeast Asians, still ineligible for citizenship).

Philippines granted independence, and a quota of 100. India also given quota of 100.

1947 Operation Bootstrap in Puerto Rico sets the stage for the "great migration" of the 1950s.

Newly formed Pakistan granted quota of 100.

1948 Displaced Persons Act permits 205,000 European war refugees to enter over two years.

Exchange Visitor Program brings Filipina nurses to study in the United States

1949 CIA created and granted a quota of 100 to bring in aliens useful to "the national mission" without regard to admissibility.[2]

1952 Immigration and Nationality Act (McCarran-Walter Act) technically eliminates race as a bar to immigration or citizenship. Asiatic barred zone abolished. Japan's quota set at 185 annually. China's remains at 105; other Asian countries given 100. Colonial subjects not eligible for quotas (e.g., black West Indians cannot enter under Britain's quota even though they are British citizens).

H-2 temporary visa establishes a large but generally ignored guest-worker program.

Attorney general is authorized to "parole" immigrants over quota for reasons of "public interest." This provision will be used for Hungarians fleeing the Soviet invasion in 1956, for 15,000 Chinese fleeing China's 1949 Communist revolution, and for 145,000 Cubans fleeing the 1959 revolution there, as well as 400,000 Southeast Asian refugees between 1975 and 1980.

Prohibition on "subversives" (and specifically Communists, anarchists, and homosexuals)

means many foreign intellectuals cannot travel to United States.

1953 Refugee Relief Act expands Displaced Persons Act of 1948 to allow 200,000 more entrants above quotas. "Refugee" defined as a person fleeing a Communist country or the Middle East. Asians allowed as refugees for the first time.

1954 "Operation Wetback" deports one million undocumented Mexicans.

Numbers entering under the Bracero program increase from 200,000 a year prior to Operation Wetback to 450,000 a year by the end of the 1950s.

1957 Refugee admissions no longer subject to quota system.

1959 Cuban Revolution; U.S. attorney general grants Cuban immigrants widespread parole to enter the United States as refugees.

Hawaii becomes a state, significantly increasing "Asian" population of U.S.

1962 Cuban Refugee Program provides financial assistance to Cuban entrants.

1964 Bracero program abolished.

1965 Hart-Celler Act establishes a uniform quota of 20,000 per country for countries outside the Western Hemisphere and a ceiling of 120,000 for immigrants from the Western Hemisphere. Family reunification, job skills, and refugee status are privileged. Immediate family members exempted from quota. Provisions made for 17,400 refugees per year.

H-2 temporary worker program continued.

Voting Rights Act strengthens citizenship for African Americans.

1966 Cuban Adjustment Act offers Cubans automatic refugee and legal permanent residence status, chargeable to the Western Hemisphere quota.

1975 Indochina Migration and Refugee Assistance Act provides resettlement assistance for refugees from Cambodia and Vietnam (Laos added in 1976).

1976 Uniform quota of 20,000 applied to Western Hemisphere countries (Cuban refugees not charged to quota system).

1977 Indochinese refugees granted permanent resident status.

1978 Eastern and Western Hemisphere quotas combined to allow 290,000 global limit.

1980 Refugee Act brings U.S. law into compliance with UN Refugee Convention (which the U.S. signed in 1968). Allows entrance to 50,000 refugees a year outside of the quota system. Defines refugees as persons who have a "well-founded fear of persecution" based on "race, religion, nationality, membership in a particular social group, or political opinion." Establishes federal programs for resettlement. Lowers global (non-refugee) quota to 270,000 a year.

Registered nurses granted special access to permanent legal status.

1981 Immigrants who are not legal permanent residents denied access to most federal aid programs.

1982 Operation Jobs—INS raids workplaces, arrests 5,000.

1986 Immigration Reform and Control Act (IRCA) allows undocumented immigrants who can prove continued presence in the country since 1982 and fulfill other requirements to apply for legalization—1.7 million apply. SAW (Special Agricultural Workers) provision allows legalization for those engaged in temporary agricultural work in 1985 and 1986. Nearly 1 million approved.

IRCA imposes employer sanctions requiring employers to verify immigration status of workers hired.

H-2 temporary worker program split between H-2A (agricultural) and H-2B (nonagricultural) workers.

1990 Global cap on immigration increased to 675,000 a year, including 480,000 family-sponsored, 140,000 employment-based, and 55,000 "diversity immigrants" from low-sending countries, especially Ireland.

American Baptist Church v. Thornburgh lawsuit settlement allows Guatemalans and Salvadorans to remain in the country and work while asylum cases are reevaluated.

1994 Operation Gatekeeper tries to close San Diego crossing points with fencing, stadium lights, and greatly increased border patrol presence. Migrant crossings start to shift eastward to the Arizona desert.

North American Free Trade Agreement (NAFTA) increases economic integration between United States and Mexico.

1996 Personal Responsibility and Work Opportunity Reconciliation Act bars legal permanent residents from most federal aid programs (food stamps, Medicaid) unless they have lived in the U.S. for five years, and allows states to create further restrictions.

Illegal Immigration Reform and Immigrant Responsibility Act (IIRAIRA) greatly increases funding for Border Patrol and detention of aliens; increases penalties for unlawful entry and facilitates deportation; requires proof of citizenship for federal public benefits; requires educational institutions to provide INS with information on foreign students. Cubans exempted from many of the provisions.

1997 Nicaraguan Adjustment and Central American Relief Act (NACARA) allows Nicaraguans and

Cubans easier access to legal permanent resident status.

2001 Uniting and Strengthening America by Providing Appropriate Tools Required to Intercept and Obstruct Terrorism (USA PATRIOT) Act prohibits entry of people associated with organizations or governments identified as supporting terrorism.

2002 Homeland Security Act replaces the Immigration and Naturalization Service (INS) with the newly created U.S. Citizenship and Immigration Services (USCIS) under the Department of Homeland Security.

ACKNOWLEDGMENTS

I'm grateful to the wonderful people who read and offered comments on the manuscript for this book at various stages of its progress: Gene Bell-Villada, David Caplan, Diane Chomsky, Rick Dionne, Ana Echevarría-Morales, Guillermo Fernández-Ampié, Julie Greene, Knut Langsetmo, Katrina Sealey, Steve Striffler, Amanda Warnock, and the students in HIS 725, Latinos in the United States, in the fall of 2006.

Many thanks to Shuya Ohno at MIRA (Massachusetts Immigrant and Refugee Advocacy Coalition) for connecting me to Gayatri Patnaik, who really deserves much of the credit for this book coming into existence at all; she and her colleagues at Beacon Press have all been a pleasure to work with.

NOTES

INTRODUCTION

1. James Loewen, *Lies My Teacher Told Me: Everything Your American History Textbook Got Wrong* (New York: Touchstone, 1995), 146, 148.
2. Jeffrey S. Passel, "The Size and Characteristics of the Unauthorized Migrant Population in the U.S.," Pew Hispanic Center, March 7, 2006, http://pewhispanic.org/files/reports/61.pdf; Steven A. Camarota, "Immigrants at Mid-Decade: A Snapshot of America's Foreign-Born Population in 2005," Center for Immigration Studies, December 2005, www.cis.org/articles/2005/back1405.html.
3. Nolan Malone, Kaali Baluja, Joseph M. Costanzo, and Cynthia J. Davis, "The Foreign-Born Population, 2000," Census 2000 brief issued December 2003, www.census.gov/prod/2003pubs/c2kbr-34.pdf.
4. Jeffrey S. Passel and Robert Suro, "Rise, Peak and Decline: Trends in U.S. Immigration 1992–2004," Pew Hispanic Center, September 27, 2005, http://pewhispanic.org/files/reports/53.pdf.
5. Immigration slowed in the 1920s, '30s, and '40s, but started to climb again, slowly, in the 1950s and '60s, and more rapidly in the 1970s and '80s. (Even though far fewer immigrants arrived in the 1920s than in previous decades, the numbers of immigrants arriving exceeded the numbers of foreign-born people who died, making 1930 the peak year.) The low point, percentage-wise, in foreign-born population was 1970, at 4.7 percent, or 9.6 million people. Numbers and percentage of the foreign born then rose, to 6.2 percent or 14.1 million people in 1980, and to 7.9 percent or 19.8 million people in 1990. See Campbell J. Gibson and Emily

Lennon, "Historical Census Statistics on the Foreign-Born Population of the United States: 1850–1990," Population Division Working Paper No. 29, February 1999, www.census.gov/population/www/documentation/twps0029/twps0029.html.

6. Arthur M. Schlesinger, *The Disuniting of America: Reflections on a Multicultural Society* (New York: Norton, 1998); Samuel P. Huntington, *Who Are We? The Challenges to America's National Identity* (New York: Simon & Schuster, 2004).
7. Quoted in Mae M. Ngai, *Impossible Subjects: Illegal Aliens and the Making of Modern America* (Princeton, NJ: Princeton University Press, 2005), 117.
8. U.S. Census Bureau, *2000 Census of the Population*, "Quick Facts: Race," http://quickfacts.census.gov/qfd/meta/long_68176.htm.
9. "Universal Declaration of Human Rights," United Nations, www.un.org/Overview/rights.html.
10. "Learn about the United States: Quick Civics Lesson," United States Citizenship and Immigration Services, www.uscis.gov/graphics/citizenship/flashcards/M-638.pdf.
11. See Christian Joppke, "The Evolution of Alien Rights in the United States, Germany, and the European Union," in *Citizenship Today: Global Perspectives and Practices*, ed. T. Alexander Aleinikoff and Douglas Klusmeyer (Washington, DC: Carnegie Endowment for International Peace, 2001), 36–62, esp. 38–44.
12. Ron Hayduk, *Democracy for All: Restoring Immigrant Voting Rights in the United States* (New York: Routledge, 2006), 3–4.
13. Ron Hayduk and Michele Wuker, "Immigrant Voting Rights Receive More Attention," Migration Information Network, November 1, 2004, www.migrationinformation.org/Feature/display.cfm?id=265.
14. Hayduk, *Democracy for All*, 4.
15. Joaquín Avila, "Political Apartheid in California: Consequences of Excluding a Growing Non-Citizen Population," UCLA Chicano Studies Research Center, *Latino Policy and Issues Brief* 9, December 2003, www.chicano.ucla.edu/press/siteart/LPIB_09Dec2003.pdf.

MYTH 1: IMMIGRANTS TAKE AMERICAN JOBS

1. F. Froebel, J. Heinrichs, and O. Krey, *The New International Division of Labour* (Cambridge, UK: Cambridge University Press, 1980).
2. In the 1980s dozens of states, from Connecticut to Florida to Oregon, established enterprise zones in economically distressed areas, offering businesses tax and other incentives to locate there. For some analyses of these efforts, see the bibliography by the U.S. Department of Housing and Urban Development, "Enterprise Zones: Case Studies and State Reports," www.huduser.org/publications/polleg/ez_bib/ez_bib3.html.
3. Rakesh Kochhar, "Growth in the Foreign-Born Workforce and Employment of the Native Born," Pew Hispanic Center, August 10, 2006, http://pewhispanic.org/reports/report.php?ReportID=69.
4. U.S. Census, "U.S. International Trade in Goods and Services," April, 2006. www.census.gov/foreign-trade/Press-Release/2006pr/04/ftdpress.txt.
5. U.S. Bureau of Labor Statistics, "Employment Status of the Civilian Non-Institutional Population, 1940 to Date," ftp://ftp.bls.gov/pub/special.requests/lf/aat1.txt or www.bls.gov/cps/cpsaat1.pdf.

MYTH 2: IMMIGRANTS COMPETE WITH LOW-SKILLED WORKERS AND DRIVE DOWN WAGES

1. Steven Greenhouse and David Leonhardt, "Real Wages Fail to Match a Rise in Productivity," *New York Times*, August 28, 2006.
2. The National Center for Public Policy and Higher Education found college costs increased sharply with respect to average income in the previous decade, so that in 2006 the cost of sending a child to college was over 30 percent of an average family income. See "Measuring Up 2006: The National Report Card on Higher Education," September 7, 2006, http://measuringup.highereducation.org/. See also Christian E. Weller, "Drowning in Debt: America's Middle Class Falls Deeper in Debt as Income Growth Slows and Costs Climb," Center for American Progress, May 2006, www.americanprogress.org/kf/boomburden-web.pdf.

3. Robert Frank, "U.S. Led a Resurgence Last Year Among Millionaires Worldwide," *Wall Street Journal*, June 15, 2004.
4. Esther Cervantes, "Immigrants and the Labor Market: What Are 'The Jobs that Americans Won't Do'?" *Dollars and Sense*, May–June 2006, 31.
5. This remark was widely reported, and widely criticized, in the United States. See "Mexican Leader Criticized for Comment on Blacks," May 15, 2005, http://edition.cnn.com/2005/US/05/14/fox.jackson/.
6. Sociologist Michael Piore gave the classic description of this phenomenon among early-twentieth-century European immigrants in *Birds of Passage* (Cambridge, MA: Cambridge University Press, 1979).
7. Doris Meissner, "U.S. Temporary Worker Programs: Lessons Learned," Migration Information Source, March 1, 2004, www.migrationinformation.org/Feature/display.cfm?ID=205.
8. Nancy Folbre, *The Invisible Heart: Economics and Family Values* (New York: New Press, 2001); Barbara Ehrenreich and Arlie Russell Hochschild, "Introduction," in *Global Woman: Nannies, Maids, and Sex Workers in the New Economy* (New York: Metropolitan Books, 2003), 7–9.
9. Bruce Western, Vincent Schiraldi, and Jason Ziedenberg, "Education and Incarceration," Justice Policy Institute, 2003, www.justicepolicy.org/downloads/EducationandIncarceration1.pdf. See also Ira Glasser, "Drug Busts=Jim Crow," *The Nation*, July 10, 2006, 24–26.
10. "Felony Disenfranchisement Laws in the United States," The Sentencing Project, April 2006, www.sentencingproject.org/pdfs/1046.pdf.

MYTH 3: UNIONS OPPOSE IMMIGRATION BECAUSE IT HARMS THE WORKING CLASS

1. Kim Moody uses this phrase in "Global Capital and Economic Nationalism: Protectionism or Solidarity?" *Against the Current*, 2000, www.solidarity-us.org/node/951.

2. William D. Haywood, *Bill Haywood's Book: The Autobiography of William D. Haywood* (New York, 1929), 181. Cited in David Roediger, *Working Toward Whiteness: How America's Immigrants Became White: The Strange Journey from Ellis Island to the Suburbs* (New York: Basic Books, 2005), 121.
3. Gompers, "Talks on Labor," *American Federationist* 12 (September 1905), 636–37, cited in Roediger, *Working Toward Whiteness*, 87.
4. Roediger, *Working Toward Whiteness*, 80, citing Andrew Neather, "Popular Republicanism, Americanism and the Roots of Anti-Communism, 1890–1925" (PhD diss., Duke, 1993), 242; Henry White, "Immigration Restriction as a Necessity," *American Federationist* 17 (April 1910), 302–304.
5. Peter Kwong, *Forbidden Workers: Illegal Chinese Immigrants and American Labor* (New York: New Press, 1997), 147.
6. Philip S. Foner, *U.S. Labor Movement and Latin America: A History of Workers' Response to Intervention* (South Hadley, MA: Bergin and Garvey, 1988), 28–29.
7. Samuel Gompers, "Imperialism—Its Dangers and Wrongs," Anti-Imperialism in the United States, 1898–1935 (Jim Zwick, website ed.), www.boondocksnet.com/ai/ailtexts/gompers.html.
8. Vernon M. Briggs, Jr., "American Unionism and U.S. Immigration Policy," Digital Commons at ILR, Cornell University (backgrounder, Center for Immigration Studies, 2001, 1–11), http://digitalcommons.ilr.cornell.edu/hr/22, 1.
9. Roediger, *Working Toward Whiteness*, 84.
10. Kwong, *Forbidden Workers*, 141.
11. Rogin, *Blackface, White Noise: Jewish Immigrants in the Hollywood Melting Pot* (Berkeley: University of California Press, rpr. ed. 1998), 57.
12. Kwong, *Forbidden Workers*, 141.
13. Rogin, *Blackface, White Noise*, 57.
14. Herbert Hill, "Racism within Organized Labor: A Report of Five Years of the AFL-CIO," *Journal of Negro Education* 30, no. 2 (Spring 1961), 109–118.
15. Kwong, *Forbidden Workers*, 152.

16. Kwong, 152–53.
17. Briggs, "American Unionism," 6.
18. Briggs, "American Unionism," 7.

MYTH 4: IMMIGRANTS DON'T PAY TAXES

1. On the growth of the informal economy in New York and other major cities in the era of globalization, see Saskia Sassen, *The Global City: New York, London, Tokyo*, 2nd ed. (Princeton, NJ: Princeton University Press, 2001), especially chaps. 8 and 9.
2. Brent Haydamack and Daniel Flaming, "Hopeful Workers, Marginal Jobs: LA's Off-the-Books Labor Force," Economic Roundtable, with Pascale Joassart, December 2005, synopsis available at www.economicrt.org/summaries/hopeful_workers_marginal_jobs_synopsis.html.
3. Eduardo Porter, "Illegal Immigrants are Bolstering Social Security with Billions," *New York Times*, April 5, 2005.
4. Porter, "Illegal Immigrants are Bolstering Social Security."

MYTH 5: IMMIGRANTS ARE A DRAIN ON THE ECONOMY

1. Steven A. Camarota, "The High Cost of Cheap Labor: Illegal Immigration and the Federal Budget," Center for Immigration Studies, August 2004, 7, www.cis.org/articles/2004/fiscal.pdf.
2. Camarota, "High Cost of Cheap Labor."
3. Sarah Beth Coffey, "Undocumented Immigrants in Georgia: Tax Contributions and Fiscal Concerns," Georgia Budget and Policy Institute, January 2006, www.gbpi.org/pubs/garevenue/20060119.pdf.
4. Robin Baker and Rich Jones, "State and Local Taxes Paid in Colorado by Undocumented Immigrants," Bell Policy Center Issue Brief no. 3, June 30, 2006, www.thebell.org/pdf/IMG/Brf3taxes.pdf.
5. Thomas D. Boswell, June Nogle, Rob Paral, and Richard Langendorf, *Facts About Immigration and Asking Six Big Questions for Florida*

and Miami-Dade County, Bureau of Economic and Business Research, University of Florida, Gainesville, November 2001.

6. See Ronald D. Lee and Timothy Miller, "Immigrants and Their Descendants," Project on the Economic Demography of Interage Income Reallocation, Demography, UC Berkeley (1997); National Research Council, *The New Americans* (Washington, DC: National Academy Press, 1997), chaps. 6 and 7; Alan J. Auerbach and Philip Oreopoulos, "Generational Accounting and Immigration in the United States," University of California, Berkeley, March 1999, http://elsa.berkeley.edu/ffiburch/immigration13.pdf.
7. Jeffrey S. Passel, "Unauthorized Migrants: Numbers and Characteristics—Background Briefing for Task Force on Immigration and America's Future," Pew Hispanic Center, June 14, 2005, 31, http://pewhispanic.org/files/reports/46.pdf.
8. Passel, "Unauthorized Migrants," 34–35.
9. Passel, "Unauthorized Migrants," 42.

MYTH 6: IMMIGRANTS SEND MOST OF WHAT THEY EARN OUT OF THE COUNTRY IN THE FORM OF REMITTANCES

1. Inter-American Development Bank, "Sending Money Home: Remittances from Latin America to the U.S., 2004," www.iadb.org/exr/remittances/images/Map2004SurveyAnalysisMay_17.pdf.
2. IADB, "Sending Money Home," 1.
3. B. Lindsay Lowell and Rodolfo O. de la Garza, "The Developmental Role of Remittances in U.S. Latino Communities and in Latin American Countries," Inter-American Dialogue, June 2000, 8–9, www.iadialog.org/publications/pdf/lowell.pdf.
4. Lowell and de la Garza, "Remittances," 13.
5. Jane Collins, *Threads: Gender, Labor, and Power in the Global Apparel Industry* (Chicago: Chicago University Press, 2003).
6. Catherine Elton, "Latin America's Faulty Lifeline," MIT Center for International Studies, "Audit of Conventional Wisdom" series, March 20, 2006, http://web.mit.edu/CIS/pdf/Audit_03_06_Elton.pdf.

PART TWO: IMMIGRANTS AND THE LAW

1. Henry David Thoreau, *Civil Disobedience*, Part I, 1849, available in many editions including online at http://thoreau.eserver.org/civil1.html.
2. Satya Sagar, "U.S. Elections: Let the Whole World Vote!" ZNet, February 27, 2004, www.zmag.org/content/print_article.cfm?itemID=5049§ionID=33.

MYTH 7: THE RULES APPLY TO EVERYONE, SO NEW IMMIGRANTS NEED TO FOLLOW THEM JUST AS IMMIGRANTS IN THE PAST DID

1. Aristide R. Zolberg, *A Nation By Design: Immigration Policy in the Fashioning of America* (Cambridge: Harvard University Press, 2006).
2. Ngai, *Impossible Subjects*, 18.

MYTH 8: THE COUNTRY IS BEING OVERRUN BY ILLEGAL IMMIGRANTS

1. United Nations International Research and Training Institute for the Advancement of Women, Fact Sheet, www.un-instraw.org/en/index.php?option=content&task=blogcategory&id=76&Itemid=110; see also the Universal Declaration of Human Rights at www.unhchr.ch/udhr/lang/eng.htm.
2. Passel, "Unauthorized Migrants," 2.
3. Passel, "Unauthorized Migrants," 3; Passel, "Size and Characteristics," 4.
4. Passel, "Size and Characteristics," 1.
5. Passel, "Unauthorized Migrants," 4.
6. Passel, "Unauthorized Migrants," 9.
7. Bill Ong Hing, *Defining America through Immigration Policy* (Philadelphia: Temple University Press, 2004), 200.
8. Passel, "Unauthorized Migrants," 9.
9. Passel, "Size and Characteristics," 6–7.

10. Passel, "Unauthorized Migrants," 26.
11. Passel, "Unauthorized Migrants," 27.
12. See Aviva Chomsky, *Linked Labor Histories* (Durham, NC: Duke University Press), forthcoming.
13. Lance Compa, "Blood, Sweat, and Fear: Workers' Rights in U.S. Meat and Poultry Processing Plants," Human Rights Watch, 2004, 12, www.hrw.org/reports/2005/usa0105/usa0105.pdf.
14. Compa, "Blood, Sweat, and Fear," 16.

MYTH 9: THE UNITED STATES HAS A GENEROUS REFUGEE POLICY

1. Sample questions are provided on the U.S. Citizenship and Immigration Services website: www.uscis.gov/graphics/citizenship/flashcards/Flashcard_questions.pdf.
2. David W. Haines, ed., *Refugees in America in the 1990s: A Reference Handbook* (Westport, CT: Greenwood Press, 1996), 3.
3. Roger Daniels, *Guarding the Golden Door: American Immigration Policy and Immigrants Since 1882* (New York: Hill and Wang, 2004), 71–87.
4. Haim Genizi, *America's Fair Share: The Admission and Resettlement of Displaced Persons, 1945–1952* (Detroit: Wayne State University Press, 1993). See also Daniels, *Guarding the Golden Door*, chaps. 3–5, for numerous examples of the overt and covert restrictions against Jews.
5. Daniels, *Guarding the Golden Door*, 108–110.
6. Ong Hing, *Defining America*, 245–47.
7. Alejandro Portes and Alex Stepick, *City on the Edge: The Transformation of Miami* (Berkeley: University of California Press, 1994), 51.
8. Ong Hing, *Defining America*, 247; Portes and Stepick, *City on the Edge*, 52.
9. Howard W. French, "Between Haiti and the U.S. Lies a Quandary," *New York Times*, November 24, 1991.
10. Anthony DePalma, "For Haitians, Voyage to a Land of Inequality," *New York Times*, July 16, 1991.

11. DePalma, "For Haitians, Voyage to a Land of Inequality."
12. Portes and Stepick, *City on the Edge*, 53.
13. Barbara Crossette, "Court Halts Expulsion of Haitians as Hundreds More Leave for U.S.," *New York Times*, November 20, 1991.
14. Paul Farmer, *The Uses of Haiti* (Monroe, ME: Common Courage Press, 1994), 270.
15. Farmer, *Uses of Haiti*, 270–71, citing Cathy Powell, " 'Life' at Guantánamo: The Wrongful Detention of Haitian Refugees," *Reconstruction* 2, no. 2 (1993), 58–68.
16. Roberto Suro, "U.N. Refugee Agency Says U.S. Violates Standards in Repatriating Haitians," *Washington Post*, January 11, 1995.
17. Farmer, *Uses of Haiti*, 273.
18. Daniel Williams, "Suddenly, the Welcome Mat Says 'You're Illegal,' " *Washington Post*, August 20, 1994.
19. "12,000 Remain at Guantánamo," *Washington Post*, August 19, 1995.
20. "U.S. Policy Changed with Guantánamo Safe Havens," *Washington Post*, February 5, 1995.
21. Bob Herbert, "In America, Suffering the Children," *New York Times*, May 27, 1995.
22. For a detailed account of these events, see María Cristina García, *Seeking Refuge: Central American Migration to Mexico, the United States, and Canada* (Berkeley: University of California Press, 2006).
23. Michael McBride, "Migrants and Asylum Seekers: Policy Responses in the United States to Immigrants and Refugees from Central America and the Caribbean," *International Migration* 37, no. 1 (March 1999), 296.
24. Ong Hing, *Defining America*, 239, 250.
25. Jay Matthews, "500,000 Immigrants Granted Legal Status: A Milestone for Central American Refugees," *Washington Post*, December 20, 1990.
26. Ong Hing, *Defining America*, 249, 254.

MYTH 10: THE UNITED STATES IS A MELTING POT THAT HAS ALWAYS WELCOMED IMMIGRANTS FROM ALL OVER THE WORLD

1. I'm referring here to HR 4437 of 2005, which criminalized and imposed mandatory sentences on those who provided aid or services that helped an immigrant to enter or remain in the United States. Almost any kind of humanitarian or social service to an undocumented immigrant could have been prosecuted under this provision.
2. James Loewen, *Sundown Towns: A Hidden Dimension of American Racism* (New York: New Press, 2005), 25.
3. "Back in the Day: Indiana's African-American History," *The Indianapolis Star*, February 2002, www2.indystar.com/library/factfiles/history/black_history/.
4. Zolberg, *Nation by Design*, 120–24 [quote from p. 124].
5. *Scott v. Sandford*, 60 U.S. 393, 407, www.law.cornell.edu/supct/html/historics/USSC_CR_0060_0393_ZO.html.
6. *Scott v. Sandford*, 410.
7. Ian F. Haney López, *White by Law: The Legal Construction of Race.* (New York: NYU Press, 1996), 39.
8. Zolberg, *Nation by Design*, 192.
9. Marian L. Smith, " 'Any woman who is now, or who may hereafter be married' . . . Women and Naturalization, ca. 1802–1940," *Prologue Magazine* [published by The National Archives] 30, no. 2 (Summer 1998), www.archives.gov/publications/prologue/1998/summer/women-and-naturalization-1.html; Haney López, *White by Law*, 128.
10. Haney López, *White by Law*, 91.
11. Ngai, *Impossible Subjects*, 22–23.
12. Ngai, *Impossible Subjects*, 26.
13. See critique in PR Newswire, "Hidden Facts in the New Census Hispanic Data," *Puerto Rico Herald*, June 13, 2005.
14. The list is reproduced in Ngai, *Impossible Subjects*, 28–29.
15. Haney López, *White by Law*, 42–45.
16. Ngai, *Impossible Subjects*, 7–8.
17. The phrase was originally coined by Rayford Logan in *The Negro in*

American Life and Thought: The Nadir in 1954. James Loewen decries its loss and tries to re-highlight it in *Sundown Towns*, chap. 2.

18. Dan Baum, "The Lottery: Once You Have a Green Card, What Next?" *The New Yorker*, January 23, 2006, www.newyorker.com/fact/content/articles/060123fa_fact.
19. "2007 DV Lottery Instructions," United States Department of State, http://travel.state.gov/visa/immigrants/types/types_1318.html.

MYTH 11: SINCE WE ARE ALL THE DESCENDANTS OF IMMIGRANTS HERE, WE ALL START ON EQUAL FOOTING

1. George Benton Adams, "The United States and the Anglo-Saxon Future," *Atlantic Monthly* 78 (1896), 35–45; quotes from pp. 36, 44.
2. John Fiske, "Manifest Destiny," Project Gutenberg, 2003, www.gutenberg.org/files/10112/10112.txt.
3. Josiah Strong, *Our Country: Its Possible Future and its Present Crisis* (Astor Place, NY: American Home Missionary Society, 1885), www.questia.com/PM.qst?a=o&d=11531335; "Josiah Strong on Anglo-Saxon Predominance, 1891," www.mtholyoke.edu/acad/intrel/protected/strong.htm.
4. David Roediger and James R. Barrett, "Inbetween Peoples: Race, Nationality, and the 'New Immigrant' Working Class," *Journal of American Ethnic History* 16, no. 3 (Spring 1997), 3–45; Roediger, *Working Toward Whiteness*; Noel Ignatiev, *How the Irish Became White* (New York: Routledge, 1995).
5. David G. Gutiérrez, *Walls and Mirrors: Mexican Americans, Mexican Immigrants, and the Politics of Ethnicity* (Berkeley: University of California Press, 1995), 14–16.
6. Camille Guerin-González, *Mexican Workers and American Dreams: Immigration, Repatriation, and California Farm Labor, 1900–1939* (New Brunswick, NJ: Rutgers University Press, 1996), 26.
7. Juan González, *Harvest of Empire: A History of Latinos in America* (New York: Penguin), 100.
8. Ngai, *Impossible Subjects*, 54.
9. Gutiérrez, *Walls and Mirrors*, 21.

10. Arnoldo de León, *They Called Them Greasers: Anglo Attitudes Towards Mexicans in Texas, 1821–1900* (Austin: University of Texas Press, 1983), 3.
11. Guerin-González, *Mexican Workers*, 29.
12. Ngai, *Impossible Subjects*, 64.
13. Ong Hing, *Defining America*, 120.
14. Vernon M. Briggs, Jr., "Guestworker Programs: Lessons from the Past and Warnings for the Future," Center for Immigration Studies, March 2004, www.cis.org/articles/2004/back304.html.
15. Ngai, *Impossible Subjects*, 72; Guerin González, *Mexican Workers*, 111.
16. Ruth Ellen Wassem and Geoffrey K. Collver, "RL 30852: Immigration of Agricultural Guest Workers: Policies, Trends, and Legislative Issues," Congressional Research Service Report for Congress, February 15, 2001, http://ncseonline.org/NLE/CRSreports/Agriculture/ag-102.cfm.
17. Ong Hing, *Defining America*, 130.
18. Ong Hing, *Defining America*, 131.
19. Wassem and Collver, "RL 30852."
20. Jeffrey S. Passel, "Estimates of the Size and Characteristics of the Undocumented Population," March 21, 2005, 6, http://pewhispanic.org/files/reports/44.pdf.
21. "Nativity of the Population, for Regions, Division, and State, 1850–1990" (table), U.S. Census Bureau, March 9, 1999, www.census.gov/population/www/documentation/twps0029/tab13.html.
22. "Population by State and U.S. Citizenship Status, With Percentages by U.S. Citizenship Status, 2003" (table), U.S. Census Bureau, www.census.gov/population/socdemo/foreign/ST023/tab1-17a.xls.
23. Camarota, "Immigrants at Mid-Decade."

MYTH 12: TODAY'S IMMIGRANTS THREATEN THE NATIONAL CULTURE BECAUSE THEY ARE NOT ASSIMILATING

1. Toni Morrison, "On the Backs of Blacks," *Time* (special issue, "The New Face of America"), December 2, 1993, www.time.com/time/community/morrisonessay.html.

2. Piri Thomas, *Down These Mean Streets* (New York: Vintage Books, 1991 [1967]), 24–27.
3. Loewen, *Sundown Towns*, 88.
4. Alex Stepick, Guillermo Grenier, Max Castro, and Marvin Dunn, *This Land Is Our Land: Immigrants and Power in Miami* (Berkeley: University of California Press, 2003), 122.
5. Marcelo Suárez-Orozco and Carola Suárez-Orozco, *Transformations: Immigration, Family Life, and Achievement Motivation among Latino Adolescents* (Stanford, CA: Stanford University Press, 1995), 60. Stepick et al. describe the same phenomenon among Haitian immigrants in Miami in *This Land Is Our Land.*
6. Jay P. Greene and Marcus A. Winters, "Public School Graduation Rates in the United States," Manhattan Institute for Public Policy Research, Civic Report 31, November 2002, www.manhattan-institute.org/html/cr_31.htm. See also Gary Orfield, ed., *Dropouts in America: Confronting the Graduation Rate Crisis* (Cambridge, MA: Harvard Education Press, 2004).
7. Pew Hispanic Center and the Henry J. Kaiser Family Foundation, "Survey Brief: Bilingualism," Pew Hispanic Center, March 2004, http://pewhispanic.org/files/reports/15.9.pdf.
8. "Poverty Status of the Population in 2003 by Sex, Age, and Hispanic Origin Type: 2004" (table), U.S. Census Bureau, www.census.gov/population/socdemo/hispanic/ASEC2004/2004CPS_tab14.2a.html.
9. Mary C. Waters, *Black Identities: West Indian Immigrant Dreams and Immigrant Realities* (New York: Russell Sage Foundation, 1999), 5.

MYTH 13: TODAY'S IMMIGRANTS ARE NOT LEARNING ENGLISH, AND BILINGUAL EDUCATION JUST ADDS TO THE PROBLEM

1. Calvin Veltman, "The Status of the Spanish Language in the United States at the Beginning of the 21st Century," *International Migration Review* 24, no. 1 (Spring 1990), 108–123. Even among four-year-olds, children of Spanish speakers tend to have significantly higher levels of English than their parents; by their teenage years, almost all children born in the United States are fluent in English (p. 113).

2. Hyon B. Shin and Rosalind Bruno, "Language Use and English-Speaking Ability: 2000," Census 2000 Brief, issued October 2003, 2, www.census.gov/prod/2003pubs/c2kbr-29.pdf.
3. Calvin Veltman, "Modelling the Language Shift Process of Hispanic Immigrants," *International Migration Review* 22, no. 4 (Winter 1988), 549.
4. Richard Alba, John Logan, Amy Lutz, and Brian Stults, "Only English by the Third Generation? Loss and Preservation of the Mother Tongue Among the Grandchildren of Contemporary Immigrants," *Demography* 39, no. 3. (August 2002), 273.
5. James Thomas Tucker, "Waiting Times for Adult ESL Classes and the Impact on English Learners," NALEO (National Association of Latino Elected and Appointed Officials) Education Fund, June 2006, 3–4, http://renewthevra.civilrights.org/resources/ESL.pdf.
6. Pew Hispanic Center Fact Sheet, "Hispanic Attitudes Toward Learning English," June 7, 2006, http://pewhispanic.org/files/factsheets/20.pdf.
7. See the U.S. English, Inc. website at www.us-english.org/inc/.
8. See www.onenation.org/fulltext.html for the texts of several of these laws.
9. James Cummins, "The Role of Primary Language Development in Promoting Educational Success for Language Minority Students," in *Schooling and Language Minority Students: A Theoretical Framework*, ed. C. F. Leyba (Los Angeles, CA: Evaluation, Dissemination and Assessment Center, California State University Los Angeles, 1981), 3–49.
10. See, for example, the recent comprehensive study funded by the U.S. Department of Education: Diane August and Timothy Shanahan, eds., *Developing Literacy in Second-Language Learners: Report of the National Literacy Panel on Language-Minority Children and Youth* (Mahwah, NJ: Lawrence Erlbaum Associates, 2006). See also J. D. Ramirez, S. D. Yuen, D. R. Ramey, and D. Pasta, *Longitudinal Study of Structured English Immersion Strategy, Early-Exit and Late-Exit Transitional Bilingual Education Programs for Language Minority: Final Report, vols. 1 and 2* (San Mateo, CA: Aguirre International,

1991), and Stephen Krashen and Grace McField, "What Works? Reviewing the Latest Evidence on Bilingual Education," *Language Learner*, November–December 2005, 7–10, 34, http://users.rcn.com/crawj/langpol/Krashen-McField.pdf.

11. Rafael M. Díaz, "Thought and Two Languages: The Impact of Bilingualism on Cognitive Development," *Review of Research on Education* 10 (1983), 23–54; Kenji Hakuta, "Degree of Bilingualism and Cognitive Ability in Mainland Puerto Rican Children," *Child Development* 58, no. 5 [Special Issue on Schools and Development] (October 1987), 1372–1388; Kenji Hakuta, *Mirror on Language: The Debate on Bilingualism* (New York: Basic Books, 1986).
12. James Crawford, "Hard Sell: Why Is Bilingual Education So Unpopular with the American Public?" Arizona State University Language Policy Research Unit, 2003, www.asu.edu/educ/epsl/LPRU/features/brief8.htm.
13. Crawford, "Hard Sell."
14. Sarah Means Lohmann and Don Soifer, "Separate Unequal Classes Set Bilingual Education Back," *Chicago Sun-Times*, May 17, 2005.
15. Crawford, "Hard Sell."
16. James Crawford, *Hold Your Tongue: Bilingualism and the Politics of English Only* (Reading, MA: Addison-Wesley, 1992), chap. 8. Excerpt online at http://ourworld.compuserve.com/homepages/JWCRAWFORD/HYTCH8.htm.

MYTH 14: IMMIGRANTS ONLY COME HERE BECAUSE THEY WANT TO ENJOY OUR HIGHER STANDARD OF LIVING

1. My discussion here draws on the work of Saskia Sassen, Douglas S. Massey, and others. Sassen's argument is accessibly summarized in "Why Immigration?" *NACLA Report on the Americas* 26, no. 1 (July 1992), pp. 14–19, Massey's in "Closed-Door Policy: Mexico Vividly Illustrates How U.S. Treatment of Immigrant Workers Backfires," *American Prospect*, July 1, 2003, www.prospect.org/print/V14/7/massey-d.html.
2. Victor Clark, cited in José-Manuel Navarro, *Creating Tropical Yan-*

kees: Social Science Textbooks and U.S. Ideological Control in Puerto Rico, 1898–1908 (New York: Routledge, 2002), 48.

3. García Ramis, *Happy Days, Uncle Sergio,* trans. Carmen C. Esteves (Fredonia, NY: White Pine Press, 1995), 33–34.
4. García Ramis, *Happy Days,* 55.
5. García Ramis, *Happy Days,* 153.
6. Quoted in Catherine Ceniza Choy, *Empire of Care: Nursing and Migration in Filipino History* (Durham, NC: Duke University Press, 2003), 86.
7. Quoted in Choy, *Empire of Care,* 102.
8. See Tim Kane, "Global Troop Deployment, 1950–2005," Heritage Foundation, www.heritage.org/Research/NationalSecurity/cda06-02.cfm. The Guantánamo naval base in Cuba is a particularly glaring example of a long-term troop presence in defiance of the "host" country's opposition.
9. Medea Benjamin and Elvia Alvarado, *Don't Be Afraid, Gringo: A Honduran Woman Speaks from the Heart* (San Francisco: Institute for Food and Development Policy, 1987), xviii-xix.
10. Chalmers Johnson, *The Sorrows of Empire: Militarism, Secrecy, and the End of the Republic* (New York: Metropolitan Books, 2004), 1, 23.
11. Sarah J. Mahler, *American Dreaming: Immigrant Life on the Margins* (Princeton, NJ: Princeton University Press, 1995), chap. 4; Roger N. Lancaster, *Life Is Hard: Machismo, Danger, and the Intimacy of Power in Nicaragua* (Berkeley: University of California Press, 1992), esp. chap. 1.
12. Quoted in Avi Chomsky, "Innocents Abroad: Taking U.S. College Students to Cuba," *LASA Forum* 27, no. 3 (Fall 1996), 16–20; quote from p. 19.
13. These and many other useful statistics have been compiled by the CIA. See www.cia.gov/cia/publications/factbook/docs/rankorder guide.html.
14. Dan Baum, "Lottery."
15. García Ramis, *Happy Days,* 14.
16. Massey, "Closed-Door Policy."
17. John Barrett, "The Cuba of the Far East," *North American Review*

164, February 1897, 173, 177, http://cdl.library.cornell.edu/cgi-bin/moa/moa-cgi?notisid=ABQ7578-0164-19.

18. For comparison's sake, U.S. investment in Central America was valued at $21 million in 1897. Walter Lafeber, *Inevitable Revolutions: The United States in Central America* (New York: Norton, 1993), 35.
19. Barrett, "Cuba of the Far East," 178.
20. Available in many sources, including Rudyard Kipling, "The White Man's Burden: The United States & The Philippine Islands, 1899," in *Rudyard Kipling's Verse: Definitive Edition* (Garden City, NY: Doubleday, 1929); online at www.historymatters.gmu.edu/d/5478/.
21. Quincy Ewing, "An Effect of the Conquest of the Philippines," Anti-Imperialism in the United States, 1898–1935 (Jim Zwick, website ed.), July 3, 2006, www.boondocksnet.com/ai/kipling/ewing.html.
22. Ngai, *Impossible Subjects*, 110.
23. Alfred Beveridge, "The March of the Flag," speech, September 16, 1898, www.fordham.edu/halsall/mod/1898beveridge.html.
24. Benjamin R. Tillman, " 'The White Man's Burden' as Prophecy," Anti-Imperialism in the United States, 1898–1935 (Jim Zwick, website ed.), www.boondocksnet.com/ai/kipling/tillman.html.
25. John Barrett, "The Problem of the Philippines," *North American Review* 167, no. 502 (September 1898), http://cdl.library.cornell.edu/cgi-bin/moa/moa-cgi?notisid=ABQ7578–0167–26.
26. Ngai, *Impossible Subjects*, 100.
27. Ngai, *Impossible Subjects*, 99.
28. Quoted in Karl Stephen Herrman, *From Yauco to Las Marías*, Project Gutenberg, www.gutenberg.org/files/10439/10439.txt.
29. Ngai, *Impossible Subjects*, 101–102.
30. James A. Tyner, "The Geopolitics of Eugenics and the Exclusion of Philippine Immigrants from the United States," *Geographical Review* 89, no. 1 (January, 1999), 63.
31. Tyner, "Geopolitics of Eugenics," 65.
32. Tyner, "Geopolitics of Eugenics," 65.
33. Ngai, *Impossible Subjects*, 119.
34. Cited in Tyner, "Geopolitics of Eugenics," 68.

35. Ngai, *Impossible Subjects*, 120.
36. Ngai, *Impossible Subjects*, 115.
37. Somini Sengupta, "The Color of Love: Removing a Relic of the Old South," *New York Times*, November 5, 2000; Somini Sengupta, "Marry at Will," *New York Times*, November 12, 2000.
38. Ngai, *Impossible Subjects*, 115.
39. Tyner, "Geopolitics of Eugenics," 67.
40. Tyner, "Geopolitics of Eugenics," 67.
41. See Aviva Chomsky, *West Indian Workers and the United Fruit Company in Costa Rica, 1870–1940* (Baton Rouge: Louisiana State University Press, 1996).
42. U.S. Library of Congress, Federal Research Division, *The Philippines: A Country Study* (Washington, DC: GPO, 1991), http://countrystudies.us/philippines/23.htm.
43. Library of Congress, *The Philippines*, http://countrystudies.us/philippines/77.htm.
44. Choy, *Empire of Care*, chaps. 1–2.
45. Choy, *Empire of Care*, 75.
46. Daniels, *Guarding the Golden Door*, 165.
47. Choy, *Empire of Care*, 96.
48. Library of Congress, *The Philippines*, http://countrystudies.us/philippines/24.htm.
49. Choy, *Empire of Care*, 13.
50. Choy, *Empire of Care*, 2.
51. Celia W. Dugger, "U.S. Plan to Lure Nurses May Hurt Poor Nations," *New York Times*, May 24, 2006.
52. This process is described in Paul Ong and Tania Azores, "The Migration and Incorporation of Filipino Nurses," in *The New Asian Immigration in Los Angeles and Global Restructuring*, ed. Paul Ong, Edna Bonacich, and Lucie Cheng (Philadelphia: Temple University Press, 1994), 165–69.
53. Ong and Azores, "Migration and Incorporation," 174–75.
54. Dugger, "Plan to Lure Nurses."
55. Dugger, "Plan to Lure Nurses."
56. Daniels, *Guarding the Golden Door*, 166.

57. Dugger, "Plan to Lure Nurses."
58. Dugger, "Plan to Lure Nurses."
59. "Filipino Remittances Hit $9.7 Billion," BBC News, http://news.bbc.co.uk/2/hi/business/4608786.stm. (The $9.7 billion figure was for the first eleven months of 2005.)
60. Dugger, "Plan to Lure Nurses."

MYTH 15: THE AMERICAN PUBLIC OPPOSES IMMIGRATION, AND THE DEBATE IN CONGRESS REFLECTS THAT

1. See the list of supporters at www.tedkennedy.com/content/177/organizations-supporting-the-kennedy-mccain-immigration-legislation.
2. See statement by the National Network for Immigrant and Refugee Rights and list of endorsers at www.nnirr.org/projects/immigrationreform/statement.htm.
3. "Statement by AFL-CIO President John J. Sweeney on President Bush's Principles for Immigration Reform," January 8, 2004, www.aflcio.org/mediacenter/prsptm/pr01082004.cfm.
4. Elizabeth Auster, "Guest Worker Proposals Divide America's Unions," *The Plain Dealer*, April 6, 2006.
5. Wayne A. Cornelius, "Controlling 'Unwanted' Immigration: Lessons from the United States, 1993–2004," *Journal of Ethnic and Migration Studies* 31, no. 4, July 2005, 788, www.ccis-ucsd.org/PUBLICATIONS/wrkg92.pdf.
6. "2006 State Legislation Related to Immigration: Enacted, Vetoed, and Pending Gubernatorial Action," National Conference of State Legislatures, July 3, 2006, www.ncsl.org/programs/immig/06ImmigEnactedLegis2.htm.
7. Bonnie Erbe, "Cities Fill Federal Void on Immigration," *Seattle Post-Intelligencer*, July 19, 2006; Mary K. Brunskill, "Pennsylvania City Passes Strict Anti-Immigration Act," *All-Headline News*, July 14, 2006; Dan Sewell, "Country's Interior Wages Own Campaign Against Illegal Aliens," Associated Press, November 22, 2005.
8. Paul Davenport, "Bill Passes Applying Trespassing Law to Illegal Immigrants," Associated Press, April 13, 2006; Jacques Belleaud,

"Governor Vetoes Attempt to Criminalize Immigrants' Presence in Arizona," Associate Press, April 18, 2006.

9. "Earned Legalization and Increased Border Security Is Key to Immigration Reform According to Republican Voters: New Poll," Manhattan Institute for Policy Research, October 17, 2005, www.manhattan-institute.org/html/immigration_pol_pr.htm.
10. Opinion Research Corporation, CNN poll, June 8–11, 2006, www.cnn.com/2006/images/06/21/lou.dobbs.tonight.poll.results.pdf.
11. Lou Dobbs, *Exporting America: Why Corporate Greed Is Shipping American Jobs Overseas* (New York: Warner Business Books, 2004), http://unionshop.aflcio.org/shop/product1.cfm?SID=1&Product_ID=496.
12. Jack Shierenbeck, "The New Lou Dobbs: Working Chumps' Champion?" *New York Teacher*, March 21, 2004.
13. Lou Dobbs, "Our Borderline Security," *U.S. News and World Report*, December 27, 2004.
14. Lou Dobbs, "Disorganized Labor," *U.S. News and World Report*, March 7, 2005.
15. Pew Research Center for People and the Press and Pew Hispanic Center, "America's Immigration Quandary: No Consensus on America's Immigration Problem or Proposed Fixes," Pew Hispanic Center, March 20, 2006, 15, http://pewhispanic.org/files/reports/63.pdf.
16. Pew Research Center, "America's Immigration Quandary," 16.
17. Pew Research Center, "America's Immigration Quandary," 18.
18. Pew Research Center, "America's Immigration Quandary," 11.
19. Teresa A. Sullivan, Elizabeth Warren, and Jay Westbrook, *The Fragile Middle Class: Americans in Debt* (New Haven: Yale University Press, 2001), 6.
20. "Government, Corporate Scandals Damage Public Trust in Institutions at the Bedrock of Society," Lichtman/Zogby interactive poll, May 23, 2006, www.zogby.com/News/ReadNews.dbm?ID=1116.
21. Michael P. McDonald and Samuel L. Popkin, "The Myth of the Vanishing Voter," *American Political Science Review* 95, no. 4 (December 2001), 963–74.

22. Pew Research Center, "America's Immigration Quandary," introduction.
23. Pew Research Center, "America's Immigration Quandary," 17, figures from CBS/*New York Times*.

MYTH 16: THE OVERWHELMING VICTORY OF PROPOSITION 187 IN CALIFORNIA SHOWS THAT THE PUBLIC OPPOSES IMMIGRATION

1. "A Summary Analysis of Voting in the 1994 General Election," California Opinion Index, January 1995, http://field.com/fieldpollonline/subscribers/COI-94-95-Jan-Election.pdf.
2. "Summary Analysis of Voting."
3. "Summary Analysis of Voting."
4. Jan Adams, "Proposition 187 Lessons," *Z Magazine*, March 1995.
5. Cornelius, "Controlling 'Unwanted' Immigration," 777, 791 n. 7.

MYTH 17: IMMIGRATION IS A PROBLEM

1. Leslie Berestein, "Migrants push east to avoid fortified border, with tragic results," *San Diego Union-Tribune*, September 29, 2004, www.signonsandiego.com/news/reports/gatekeeper/20040929-9999-lz1n29mirgran.html.
2. Mark Stevenson, "Mexico Puts Up Maps for Migrants," *Desert News*, January 25, 2006, www.findarticles.com/p/articles/mi_qn4188/is_20060125/ai_n16022823; Richard Marosi, "Border-Crossing Deaths Set a 12-Month Record," *Los Angeles Times*, October 1, 2005.
3. Esther Pan, "Q&A: Homeland Security: U.S.-Mexico Border Woes," Council on Foreign Relations, February 22, 2006, repr. *New York Times*, February 22, 2006.
4. Sonia Nazario, *Enrique's Journey* (New York: Random House, 2006), 5, xiv.
5. Laura Wides, "Study Says Immigration Patterns Changing with New Border Security," Associated Press, April 1, 2005.
6. Ong Hing, *Defining America*, 189.
7. Cornelius, "Controlling 'Unwanted' Immigration," 783.
8. Programa para el Esclaracimiento Histórico, *Guatemala: Memoria del Silencio*, Anexo I, Caso Ilustrativo 64, American Academy for

the Advancement of Science, http://shr.aaas.org/guatemala/ceh/mds/spanish/anexo1/vo11/no64.html.

9. See Pierette Hondagneu-Sotelo, *Doméstica: Immigrant Workers Cleaning and Caring in the Shadows of Affluence* (Berkeley: University of California Press, 1991), 8.
10. Berestein, "Migrants Push East."
11. James Smith, "Guatemala: Economic Migrants Replace Political Refugees," Inforpress Centroamericana, April 2006, www.migrationinformation.org/Profiles/display.cfm?ID=392.
12. See also Nora Hamilton and Norma Stoltz Chinchilla, *Seeking Community in a Global City: Guatemalans and Salvadorans in Los Angeles* (Philadelphia: Temple University Press, 2001); Gabrielle Kohlpahl, *Voices of Guatemalan Women in Los Angeles: Understanding Their Immigration* (New York: Garland, 1999).
13. Smith, "Guatemala."
14. Berestein, "Migrants Push East."

MYTH 18: COUNTRIES NEED TO CONTROL WHO GOES IN AND OUT

1. "On Indian Removal," President Andrew Jackson, message to Congress, December 6, 1830, available on many websites, including Our Documents, www.ourdocuments.gov/doc.php?flash=true&doc=25.
2. Tyner, "Geopolitics of Eugenics," 57.
3. Tyner, "Geopolitics of Eugenics," 56.
4. See Edward J. Larson, *Sex, Race, and Science: Eugenics in the Deep South* (Baltimore: Johns Hopkins University Press, 1995); Nancy L. Gallagher, *Breeding Better Vermonters: The Eugenics Project in the Green Mountain State* (Hanover, NH: University Press of New England, 1999); Bonnie Mass, "Puerto Rico: A Case Study in Population Control," *Latin American Perspectives* 4, no. 4 (Autumn 1977), 66–71.
5. Alexandra Minna Stern, "Sterilized in the Name of Public Health: Race, Immigration, and Reproductive Control in Modern California," *American Journal of Public Health* 95, no. 7 (July 2005), 1128–38.

6. Laura Briggs, *Reproducing Empire: Race, Sex, Science, and U.S. Imperialism in Puerto Rico* (Berkeley: University of California Press, 2002), 83.
7. Briggs, *Reproducing Empire*, 87.
8. Briggs, *Reproducing Empire*, 106.
9. Briggs, *Reproducing Empire*, 124.
10. Stern, "Sterilized in the Name of Public Health," 1132.
11. Stern, "Sterilized in the Name of Public Health," 1133.
12. Jane Lawrence, "The Indian Health Service and the Sterilization of Native American Women," *American Indian Quarterly* 24:3 (2000), 400–419; 410. She is citing Bernard Rosenfeld, Sidney M. Wolfe, and Robert E. McGarrah Jr., *A Health Research Group Study on Surgical Sterilization: Present Abuses and Proposed Regulations* (Washington, DC: Health Research Group, 29 October 1973), 2–7.
13. Lawrence, "The Indian Health Service and the Sterilization of Native American Women." She is citing "Killing Our Future: Sterilization and Experiments," *Akwesasne Notes* 9:1 (1977), 4–6.
14. J. J. Salvo, M. G. Powers, and R. S. Cooney, "Contraceptive Use and Sterilization Among Puerto Rican Women," *Family Planning Perspectives* 24, no. 5, (September–October 1992), 219–23.
15. Andrea P. MacKay, Burney A. Kieke, Jr., Lisa M. Koonin, and Karen Beattie, "Tubal Sterilization in the United States, 1994–1996," *Family Planning Perspectives* 33, no. 4 (July–August 2001), www.guttmacher.org/pubs/journals/3316101.html.
16. "Bennett's Take on Blacks, Abortion Draws Fire," *Los Angeles Times*, September 30, 2005, A29.
17. Daniels, *Guarding the Golden Door*, 196.
18. Laura Briggs, "Making 'American' Families: Transnational Adoption and U.S. Latin America Policy," in *Haunted By Empire*, ed. Ann Laura Stoler (Durham, NC: Duke University Press, 2006), 613.
19. Laura Briggs, "Communities Resisting Interracial Adoption: The Indian Child Welfare Act and the NABSW Statement of 1972" (paper presented at the Alliance for the Study of Adoption, Identity and Kinship (ASAIK) Conference on Adoption and Culture,

University of Tampa, Tampa, FL, November 17–20, 2005, www.u.arizona.edu/ffilbriggs/.

20. "In Daddy's Arms," *Boston Globe*, July 26, 2006. For a great collection on the politics of transracial and international adoption, see Jane Jeong Trenka, Julia Chinyere Oparah, and Sun Yung Chin, eds., *Outsiders Within: Writing on Transracial Adoption* (Boston: South End Press, 2006).

MYTH 19: WE NEED TO PROTECT OUR BORDERS TO PREVENT CRIMINALS AND TERRORISTS FROM ENTERING THE COUNTRY

1. *Terrorism: 2000–2001*, U.S. Department of Justice, Federal Bureau of Investigation (FBI Publication 0308), www.fbi.gov/publications/terror/terror2000_2001.pdf.
2. Steven A. Camarota, "The Open Door: How Militant Islamic Terrorists Entered and Remained in the United States, 1993–2001," Center for Immigration Studies, www.cis.org/articles/2002/Paper21/terrorism.html.

MYTH 20: IF PEOPLE BREAK OUR LAWS BY IMMIGRATING ILLEGALLY, THEY ARE CRIMINALS AND SHOULD BE DEPORTED

1. Julia Preston, "Rules Collide with Reality in the Immigration Debate," *New York Times*, May 29, 2006.
2. *Visa Bulletin* 8, no. 96, U.S. Department of State, August 2006, http://travel.state.gov/visa/frvi/bulletin/bulletin_2978.html. These figures are updated monthly; for links to subsequent issues, go to http://travel.state.gov/visa/frvi/bulletin/bulletin_1360.html.
3. "Detention and Death of 81-Year-Old Haitian Pastor 'Appalling' Says Humanitarian Agency Director," press release, Church World Service, November 22, 2004, www.churchworldservice.org/news/archives/2004/11/245.html.
4. Tom Miller, "Latino USA" commentary, NPR, May 5–11, 2006, audio at www.latinousa.org/program/lusapgm683.html; transcription at www.walterlippmann.com/docs608.html.

MYTH 21: THE PROBLEMS THIS BOOK RAISES ARE SO HUGE THAT THERE'S NOTHING WE CAN DO ABOUT THEM

1. For a summary of the law go to www.uscis.gov/graphics/shared/aboutus/statistics/legishist/act142.htm.
2. Eduardo Galeano, "Snapshots of a World Coming Apart at the Seams," in *Appeal to Reason: 25 Years of* In These Times, ed. Craig Aaron (New York: Seven Stories Press, 2002), 194.

EPILOGUE

1. "UN Population Report Says World Urban Population of 3 Billion Today; Expected to Reach 5 Billion by 2030," press release, United Nations Population Division, March 24, 2004, www.un.org/esa/population/publications/wup2003/pop899_English.doc.

TIMELINE

1. Descriptions of many of the laws named in this timeline can be found at www.uscis.gov/graphics/shared/aboutus/statistics/legishist/index.htm. For a narrative history of U.S. immigration policy, see Marian L. Smith, "Overview of INS History," in *A Historical Guide to the U.S. Government*, ed. George T. Kurian (New York: Oxford University Press, 1998), reproduced on the U.S. Citizenship and Immigration Service website at www.uscis.gov/graphics/aboutus/history/articles/oview.htm.
2. Daniels, *Guarding the Golden Door*, 100.